My Wayward Parent
Irvin S. Cobb

My
Wayward Parent

A Book about Irvin S. Cobb

by ELISABETH COBB

Illustrated by F. STROBEL

THE BOBBS-MERRILL COMPANY
PUBLISHERS
INDIANAPOLIS · NEW YORK

First Edition

This book was written for Laura Baker Cobb.
In her name and my father's and mine
it is dedicated to all the
old friends and dear companions.

TABLE OF CONTENTS

My Wayward Parent
Irvin S. Cobb

NOT AN INTRODUCTION BUT
INSTEAD OF ONE

THE end came in New York after such a long time of pain and weariness that when my mother called me in California to tell me that he had left us, I could feel nothing except deep relief and gladness for him, remembering with horror all that weary time in the hotel bedroom in New York where he had lain with his back hurting, and his teeth hurting, and his poor insides so swollen and aching with dropsy, when he grew so tired of lying and looking at the ceiling and trying to be a good sport about his sickness—he who once roared like a wolf at a cut finger!—with all his functions breaking down so badly that even breathing, or turning over in bed, became major problems and painful ones.

Nunnally Johnson called me that morning, very early, asking if I had seen the papers, and particularly Gene Fowler's tender little piece, and I think that I shocked him a little when I said yes, I had seen all the papers, and was just sitting down to write Mr. Fowler a note to tell him how pleased Irvin was going to be. Nunnally gave a little gasp, evidently thinking that I had not grasped the fact that my father was gone, but rallying valiantly to indulge my delusion, said: "I was thinking that myself. He's sure getting nice billing. I'm glad I know the guy who can push the war off the front pages."

"Yes," I said, "he'll be tickled pink."

It must have been a week or more before I began to use the past tense in speaking of him, and all that time there was no sense of loss, only of gladness for him.

Then at last I had to go out to our old house on the canyon at
Santa Monica. It had been closed for almost a year, and for
many reasons all of us had been glad to leave it, so now it had
the put-upon air that an abandoned house seems to wear, and
was almost visibly sulking, like an unjustly punished child. I
drove through the entrance, which has no gates but instead a
tunnel of arched cedars, very dark and green, and past the
glimpse of garden, that used fairly to blaze when my mother
worked in it all day long, and up to the turn-around, and the
wall that separates the drive from the patio, where a rose-red
bougainvillea vine was in full bloom, and stopping the car, I
sat there in the hot sun and shivered.

For when I opened the gate into the patio I knew that no one
would be there, and suddenly it was almost unbearable that this
should be so. . . . It had been very different once!

Once my kids would have been there, and if this were a usual
run-of-the-mill sort of day, Cobbie but just saved from drown-
ing in the fishpond or falling down the canyon, and Pat upstairs busy dressing like crazy for a beau, and Ivy—as the babies
called him—sitting in the patio, robed in one of those Gawd-
awful smocks of his, with a large Concho belt girdling in the
folds, a couple of pounds of Indian turquoise displayed hither
and yon about his ample person, and on his head, for the purpose of training his cowlick rain or shine, indoors, outdoors or
in my lady's chamber, a large, soft, expensive hat. Not quite a
cowboy's hat. But not quite not a cowboy's hat. *His* hat.

And his greeting?

"Now you can fix a drink for your aged and revered pa, my
child . . . and see if you can't get your mother to stop personally
carrying large trees about from place to place. She's the wonder of the world, that woman! You can't fool *her*. No, sir.
She always knows exactly when she is going to collapse from
utter exhaustion—just half an hour after it has happened!"

Then he'd rock ... rock ... rock ... squeak ... squeak ... *squeak*.

His chair wasn't a real rocker. In fact it was rather a chic contraption designed for California patios, made of twisted iron, a flat piece for the ground, bent up in front and then over into arms and a back, so that it looked pretty much like any other chair except that it had no hind parts and could be rocked, or at least its seat, and its sitter's seat, moved briskly up and down, which is a pretty fair imitation of rocking. It had very smart blue and white cushions and not a Glamour Girl in all Glamour Gulch (his name for Hollywood) but would have welcomed it to a Glamour Garden. But when Ivy sat in it it was just a rocker, just as his garden, for all the exotic glory of its flowering, with hibiscus and bougainvillea and ginger and crown-of-thorns vine, was never quite a garden, but always a yard. And the patio wasn't really a patio. It was a front porch. And, in spite of its geographical location, it did not really look out upon mountains and canyon and a pie-shaped glimpse of the Pacific Ocean. It looked out on Main Street.

That's the way our house was. Why, we never gave a dinner party in our lives! Only once in a while "some folks dropped in." My mother, having a taste for the formalities, struggled against this. She put up a pretty good battle, too, with lace and glass and eighteenth-century English walnut and old silver, and clothes from Paris, and Scotch instead of bourbon for Old Fashioneds. No use! He liked all that, too, very much. Still no use. We had come a long trip, from Savannah, Georgia, and Paducah, Kentucky, with a thirty-year stopover in New York before we got to Hollywood, but that meant nothing. As long as Ivy sat there, making the iron patio chair into a rocker, we were countryfolk whether we liked it or not. And we liked it.

Well, if this was a day like most days used to be, I'd have gone past him, grumbling that it seemed to me that he might have got out the cocktail tray for once, and, in passing, given my mother a perfunctory shouted command to stop working herself to death; perfunctory because I knew that she would pay me no mind—and in this I was cleverer than he, because he always expected that she would and was always surprised when she didn't. Then I would mix him his mild toddy, and bring it to him and he would give me the news of the day. "Your son," he'd say, "made a really valiant attempt at auto-da-fé by throwing himself off the canyon, but was preserved for reasons best known to the Deity. . . . Pat's upstairs. What's she doing?"

"Dressing to go out."

"That child! She shouldn't be going out! . . . It's ridiculous. . . . You ought to stop it."

Then, calling upstairs: "Rabbit . . . come here. . . . Let's see how you look . . . ?" His mouth would be severe, his eyes blind with love and delight, that his rabbit—"God's rabbit" as he called her—had a beau, and fun, and a pretty frock.

In a little while he would cock an eye at me. "What's good for dinner? I'm getting peckish."

And when I delivered any glad tidings from the culinary front he'd ask, "Anybody dropping in?" If there wasn't, I think he was always a little disappointed, for if someone was expected, he brisked up at once. "Well, they're nice enough folks." That was a high, and usual, compliment. After a while he'd go up to dress, first pausing to roar one last command to or at my mother: "Damn it, Lolly! *Will* you stop?"

He was a dandy in his own weird way. And weird is certainly the word. Those incredible clothes! They might be any color of the rainbow, with some leanings to bright red, purple, mustard yellow, royal blue and a peculiarly loathsome sort of grass green. Once he was under strict orders—from Laura—to buy a *plain, dark* winter overcoat. He promised. The coat was delivered and before she could get a load of it he was detected in the act of sneaking it into his closet in a hurried and furtive manner. The "plain, dark" coat had come out *that* green again! No other human being ever having been seen wearing this color, we suspected that he had not stopped with having the atrocity tailored for him. He had caused it to be *woven*. On purpose! Draped in it, he resembled an El Greco landscape illuminated by neon lights.

This was deliberate. He was so far from color-blind that he never mixed up these colors, fearful and wondrous though they were. No mean feat either, let me tell you. No, as much as they could, they all harmonized, and were all most carefully selected, were all Gawd-awful . . . and—believe it or not—all very becoming to him.

So when he came downstairs for his dinner he would be as dazzling as a Montana sunset, immaculate as a sea shell, smelling pleasantly of the best Eau de Cologne, and in an expectant frame of mind. If the guests were on time he expected to enjoy himself. If they were eight seconds late he expected to enjoy himself, too, but in a different way. At least this is what I suspect. For surely no one could get *that* mad, could command and release such roaring floods of eloquence and bad temper, without enjoying it. . . .

So . . . I sat shivering in the sun outside the closed patio gate. For the life was gone from the house now. None of us would come here again except to sell, to close, to give away, to dismantle what had been a home. At the last this place had become a burden, and in it we had all suffered unhappiness and disappointments. In the fall, in September, we had set out for New York with such excitement and anticipation. But it was hard to push the gate open all the same, and for the first time I began to feel lonely, I began to miss him.

When I finally went into the house I went straight up the stairs to his room, for that which had brought me to the house was most likely to be found there. The publishers had wired me that morning asking for the manuscript on which he had been working before he left for the East, for this was a continuation of his autobiography and they wanted it as soon as possible, with the idea of publishing a little memorial volume.

I was pretty sure that I would find it in his big bureau which was always jammed indiscriminately with shirts and ties and stuff, and odd snapshots and press clippings and tag ends of correspondence, and the "piece" on which he was currently at work.

I began to search through the bureau, with the most horrible feeling of guilt, because if he had been present I'd just as lief have pawed about among the personal belongings of a Bengal tiger. As far as anyone could see there was no system used in the packing of that bureau, but there must have been some, because he could always find anything, and instantly, while the whole order of things was destroyed for him if any guilty wretch removed as much as a two-cent stamp. Yes, that is where they were kept, not in the stamp box on his desk. This usually contained his teeth. That is, if he had remembered to put them there. But often they would be just around, somewhere or other. He used to laugh, ruefully enough, at Cobbie's delight in these fierce, enormous, roving teeth. Once, when Cobbie was about three, he was found standing looking at them with the most passionate admiration visible in his little face.

"Ivy, you have to grow up to be a big man before you can have teeth like these, don't you?" he asked wistfully.

"Yes, alas!" said Dad, and Cobbie, tugging at his own baby pearls, sighed deeply.

"Oh, dear! That is a shame. For *yours* are *so* beautiful!"

The precious manuscript was not in the bureau and I began to look around for it, briskly enough now, for the room was so changed from the way it had been when he lived in it that I did not feel so bad about taking liberties here.

When he was home, every inch of the walls was covered with specimens of his Indian collection, tomahawks, war bonnets, lances, war drums, moccasins, chief robes and some particularly treasured stone things, most perilous in aspect, which might have been more domestic implements, like corn grinders, for all I know.

He used Navajo rugs on his floor, and folded across the foot of his bed. On the night table was Charlie Russell's small bronze of a Medicine Man, and over his head hung a portrait of a rugmaker. The only place in the room not adorned with Indian relics or specimens of Indian arts and crafts, was the bookcase, and it held a small, but rare, collection of books dealing with Indians. Sunny mornings he used to spend hours and hours polishing and mending and gluing his new Indian purchases. He was fond of Indians.

Thus decorated, this room was enough to scare the boldest; nervous housemaids have been known to refuse to vacuum it, and once—but only once—I slept there. The nightmares were fierce! It always gave me a mild case of the horrors, until I said as much to Roland Young, and he told me not to be so silly, that it was just a small boy's room and the things in it no more awful than was good and right and natural. True . . . maybe! Perhaps Roland was wrong. After all, *he* collects penguins. Thousands and thousands of penguins. There is no doubt that penguins have charm. But when there are so many of them? A little scary, no?

Today the walls were bare and all the Indian relics packed away for fear of moths. But surely even the California, or sun-kissed, moth couldn't do much harm to a stone tomahawk?

Just the same it was probably reposing in jeweler's cotton!

Beside his big desk was a packing case, nailed and addressed to the Paducah Public Library, containing his own books. There were only clothes in the dressing room. No manuscript.

And then, after hours of search, I found it, in a dressmaker's box, unlabeled and thrust clear out of sight in the darkest back of a closet, with the catalogue of his Indian collection and a box full of old snapshots and family papers on top of it.

It was so typical. There must have been six or seven very smart leather portfolios and brief cases piled up in a corner, absolutely empty. He was a funny man!

Opening up that box was an emotional business. The manuscript was in longhand in the firm, very beautiful, very characteristic script, with all the elisions, corrections and additions confusing the pages but also making them so very personal, so profoundly his, as no printed pages can ever be. And no one but he had seen this work.

I sat on the floor with the box in my lap, and suddenly I thought, "Why, everything is here. All the record. In one room and a hall closet."

Here were the only clippings that he had bothered to keep . . . the story published in the Savannah paper of his marriage; his mother's obituary; a picture torn from a tabloid, of himself and Pat when she first came home from Italy as a baby; a handful of snapshots taken at the front in France in 1917; a letter or two from me; and, of all the thousands of what might be called public letters, only one—a little note from President Woodrow Wilson. Then there was a chronicle of the Cobb family from the time of their landing early in the seventeenth century in Massachusetts, the Indian catalogue, his own books in the packing box, the "piece" he had not finished. It was all here.

And it wasn't enough. There, alone, I fell into a panic at

the thought of how little there was of him. I wanted most frantically to know him better. He was my father and I his only child, and besides we had always been good companions, but just the same, and for the first time, I realized how little I knew about him.

Strange ... Here was a man whose job it had been to express himself, who had written thousands and thousands of words of fiction, and two big chunks of autobiography, with whom I had lived for much the greater part of my maturity as well as all my childhood. And I knew him not at all. I knew his eccentricities, his opinions, his wit, his habits. I could give a fair guess at how he was likely to react to any given situation.

I'd take any given bet that come what may he was never going to display any undue enthusiasm for Roosevelt. And he wasn't going overboard for Joe Stalin either. At least not so far as you could notice it. And with his build . . . you'd notice it.

And I don't think he was ever going to work up any real liking for violinists, tap dancers, caviar, crooners, lady columnists, auction bridge, wild poker, backbiters, social climbers, dinner dances, any sort or description of phony (and he had the nose of a truffle hound for the detecting of same), or people who expected him to stay up after ten o'clock.

And he was going to keep on loving the woods and his folks and a good audience, and shooting ducks, or at least aiming at them, and all simple kindly people, and all brave ones, and all men who love their country and are willing to let us love ours, in peace.

He was a great talker, voluble, explicit, eloquent. But when had I ever heard him talk about himself, as distinguished from the things that had happened to him? Only once or twice, and then it had been very difficult for him. In all those published words, there is hardly a word about the man Irvin Cobb, amid all those telling, and in the greatest detail, of his adventures and opinions.

It seemed to me that he had always hidden himself behind the safest rampart in the world—a flood of words.

I had hoped, so very much, that the contents of the dressmaker's box, his last work, and what's more, the work that he knew was going to be his last (witness that packed and addressed box of books) would be different, that at last he had spoken out about himself, his real self, the man called Irvin.

But he hadn't. I was sick with disappointment when I finished reading it all, right there where I was, seated on the floor in the dusty closet. Certainly it was interesting. Of course it was well done! He was ever a craftsman, a storyteller, but it wasn't what I had hoped to find. My father had gone, and I would never, never know him now.

Farther on you may read what I found in the dressmaker's box, but the rest of this book is a search for the man as he was, and what made him so. It seems to me that Laura, my mother, holds a twist of Ariadne's thread; a thread that may lead me to an understanding of him. That is why I call this a book for her.

When I had gone this far with this narrative I read it to my mother, and found her full of protests. There was much too much about her in it, and this was Irvin's story, and why in the world should anyone be interested in her? But I told her that I had to tell about her because Dad was twenty-three when they were married, sixty-eight when he died, and so they had lived together for forty-five years, or more than double the time that he had spent without her, and how could I tell about those forty-five years without including her? Even if he had not respected her and her ideas and her way of life, which was far from being so, the very weight of accumulated and mutually experienced time must have made some impression on him.

After all . . . forty-five years! In that time she must either have been an influence on his life—or he'd have divorced her, killed her or gone nuts.

So, ignoring Laura's faint cries from off stage, I am going right ahead and tell the story from her angle, which naturally includes her background and history.

Chapter 1

To Explain the Differences Between Two Southern Homes, One Sunny and the Other Not

IT WAS fantastic that they should ever have married each other. They had not one single thing in common, except that they both happened to be born below that mythical line called Mason and Dixon's—and, at that, they picked the extremest possible ends of it for their respective nativities, there being pretty near as much difference between St. Paul and Santa Fe, as there is between the old seacoast Georgia town of Savannah, whence came little Laura Baker, and Paducah, Kentucky, the river junction, down in the Pennyrile, with Illinois just a good stiff row in a flat-bottomed boat across the river. Both places sent their men to fight and die for the Bonnie Blue Flag. Period. Here all resemblances cease.

And even the sacred Lost Cause did not mean the same thing to these two because my mother was, and is, bored to death with those who can, or will, live only in the past, and Dad was so saturated with Civil War lore that I once accused him of believing that he had fought in it his own self, warning him to look out or he'd end like poor old George IV, who, so I hear, got himself so worked up about the Battle of Waterloo that he actually convinced himself that he had fought in it and before he died was in some confusion as to whether he was the King of England, the Duke of Wellington or, in depressed moments, Napoleon Bonaparte. At this, Dad cocked an eye, that extraordinary eye, at once so beautiful and so keen, grinned reluctantly and bade me mind my manners. Just the same, next time he fell into a reminiscent mood away we went again, charging with Pickett, or serving in the Orphan's Brigade. Well, a lot of his folks were there. As a boy, for him the biggest doings

in town happened on the evenings when he was permitted to crouch on the steps of Judge Bishop's porch, that same Judge Bishop who was later to become Judge Priest of the *Saturday Evening Post* and the movies. There, on summer nights the young Irvin would listen popeyed to the old veterans tell sad, old, brave tales. They captured his imagination so completely that no other images ever marched there as vividly as those which were clothed in gray, and fighting a lost war.

Savannah is an old and very conservative place and Paducah is a river town and, only a few short yesterdays or so ago, a frontier town. My father's grandfather was born in a log cabin, when there were still Indians—and hostile ones at that— abroad in the land, and the old gentleman, who lived to see the nineties, had never worn an overcoat in his life. An Indian blanket was enough to keep him warm, come wintertime.

Now Laura had once been led from the theater in black disgrace, because she laughed out loud in public, and Irvin had been covering the water front, or rather the river front, reporting lynchings and barroom brawls and gun fights and "sporting house" rumpuses since he was sixteen.

For it was at this advanced age that he had to turn to and help support his family, a family bound and determined to remain "Southern aristocrats" (translation: Ladies Don't Work) even if their son and brother did have to carry a man's burden on frail young shoulders. It seems that his father was starting a really spirited attempt to drink himself to death about then, and, for all his earnest attention to the project, making slow work of the job. Dad told me, long after, that for many years he had been very bitter toward his father and it was not until he himself was getting on that it had occurred to him that his father had been trying to commit suicide, but in such a way that his family might collect on his small, but desperately needed, life-insurance policy.

It took his father four years. They must have been grim enough. But if Joshua Cobb deliberately killed himself with whisky, so that his little brood might benefit, he may have died happy. For they did collect. And blew the works as quickly as possible. Then, to make things good and tough, his maternal grandfather, old Dr. Saunders, died, he who had been the mainstay, the sturdy oak, the fierce, old, proud support of all his feckless brood, and half the countryside to boot.

Dad wrote a great deal about Dr. Reuben Saunders in his autobiography, and this was only just, for he was the silent old man's favorite. They were of one blood and one spirit. As I try to reach back to the past it is the Doctor's figure that stands out the clearest, for, or so it seems to me, it was the Doctor, and he alone, who ever really thought much about the young Irvin, or planned things for him.

I may be doing the memory of Joel Shrewsbury an injustice when I say this, for Dad writes:

"Uncle Jo," more beloved to . . . us, I'd say, than had he been of blood kin. At the wedding of my father and mother he "stood up" as best man and until death divided them, he remained my father's closest friend. . . . Repeatedly he drummed it into my juvenile ears that if I hoped to grow up a true Southern gentleman, I must acquire these cardinal qualifications, to wit: Become a finished horseman (I can't recall ever seeing him on horseback), read, write and speak Latin (he couldn't speak it himself), learn to dance (he never danced), and play the fiddle (he couldn't play a note).

Perhaps it was because Uncle Joe thought he should learn to play that on a certain Christmas morning Dad was given a fiddle.

Now Christmas was a day he could just about manage to live through without blowing his topper, and that's all, and his dread of it dates back to that day. His sister Reubie had been given a diamond ring and he was given the cheapest fiddle that could be bought. And he was tone-deaf. This is the kind of hurt that no one ever forgets.

It was his grandfather who found him that morning, solitary and silent, not crying but not displaying any real Yuletide cheer either, and though the Doctor did not ask the boy any questions, nor say much, it not being his habit ever to say any more than was strictly necessary, he must have done some investigating, for late that afternoon he reappeared at the house and stamped in to announce that there was now a pony stabled out in the barn and a saddle hanging in the tack room. My grandmother was delighted. "The children will love it! . . . Imagine! . . . A pony!".

"It is not for the children," said Dr. Saunders. "It is for Irvin. Only for Irvin. Remember that, Manie."

And it was the Doctor who, seeing that the boy was looking a little peaked, first bought him a gun and then ordered that he be withdrawn from the town school and sent to one out in the country so that twice a day, perforce, he must walk long times in the good clean air of the woods. The gun was to keep him from getting bored on his long trudge to school and back. It did that, and more. It gave the boy a lifelong passion for hunting, for birds, for solitude, and for nature.

Yes, Dad lost an awful lot more than just financial help, and that included his chance to go off to school and college, when he lost the Doctor. All in all his was a childhood to mature one early, and when he married at twenty-three he was old for his age. He was always old for his age, just as my mother was born young for hers.

When my father met her she was little and dark and pretty and merry and literal-minded and conservative and easily shocked—enthusiastic, very impatient, quicksilver to move, passionately loyal, and about as nonliterary as a literate person can be. It is queer how people never do come out all of one piece. For instance, I am sure that no one reading that description of her would imagine her to be all those things, and extraordinarily psychic besides. But she is. So much so that it frightens her, and me, and when she says that she has a "hunch" about anything, I begin to lay my plans her way, because although she is the least interfering of women, I know that that is the way things are going to be.

He was big, all except his hands and feet, which were so small that the six-foot bridegroom was married in his bride's gloves, the bride having made five feet by a big effort. He had that Irish coloring of very, very white skin and very blue eyes and very black hair. Now, tinted so, are you a blond or a brunette? Long, lean, skinny, narrow-shouldered, gangling boy (yes, skinny is the word—they used to call him "Shrivly"), I guess he was about as homely a kid, except for his eyes and brow, as ever hit Kentucky since Abe Lincoln left home. She was merry, but he was a wit—and these are two very different things indeed.

I think that perhaps it is impossible to be a wit without also being essentially, deeply, and tragically, a melancholy person. He was. She is literal-minded; he was devoured by his own imagination. She was socially very conservative, he most uninhibited in his manners. . . . Just go down the list, take the word for her, then find the antithesis and that was he. In only one thing were they mated. They could both work very hard, and each respected this capacity in the other. And, oh, yes . . . they were both idolatrous parents, and they were both fantastically generous.

Well, they had all this beautiful compatibility of temperament, and eighteen dollars a week besides. How could they miss? That's what they asked themselves.

They didn't and, what's more, in their old age they knew that they hadn't, but sometimes through the middle years, being much crowded by the world, perhaps they were not so sure, especially after they got me as raised as I am ever likely to be. In the early days they could always interest themselves in a discussion as to whether I was going to be hanged officially, with due pomp and ceremony, or merely privately assassinated, but after a while, as they never agreed on this, the discussions grew sort of futile and frayed and worn out, so he took to fishing and she took to bridge, and when they did meet, between rubbers and trout seasons, wherever it was, they instantly bought a house. Out of pure nervousness, I sometimes think. . . .

Anyhow I do know this, if Irvin and Laura Cobb had been cast ashore on a desert island for many long and weary years, when the rescue ship came for them at last they would have found themselves unable to leave with it, at least not until the second mortgage was paid off on that island, and the bluestone road finished and the rose garden laid out. And what's more they never would have got their money out of that island —not if it was like the rest of their real estate, they wouldn't!

Her youth was as happy a one as his was not. Perhaps the horrors of an unhappy old age are a little dimmed by the anesthesia of failing faculties, but I think that the memories of childhood are the vividest ones we will ever know, so that anyone who was happy and loved as a child is forever armored against the worst. That person has had the best, and when every sense was quick to receive it, and when it was needed most. Anyone who has had the best has had a lot. And perhaps anyone who hasn't had the best hasn't had anything at all. Perhaps I think this because it seems to me that Irvin never had anything. Fame and money and achievement, even the loves of his maturity, were all like fairy gold and fairy food to him, and when one takes these into one's hands the gold turns to dirt, the food to dust. And you eat the dust, and eat and eat, for you are so very hungry, but it never, never nourishes you.

Now Laura's folks were sweet and loving, simple people with an established position in their own world. And although this was a small one, it was also one capable of enlarging the spirit through the cherished traditions and dignity of its past. She had a sister and a brother, and they all shared equally in their parents' affections and pocketbook. They were never punished, only prayed over when naughty. Listen—don't jump to conclusions! This was no small punishment. Hours on one's knees and not even for one's own sins! Naturally they avoided naughtiness as much as possible, or, if unavoidably led into evil, never told on one another. This makes for great harmony in family life.

The two girls were sent to a good boarding school, at some financial sacrifice to their parents, although they never knew this until long afterward, and when they came home the house in town and the little cottage by the sea were turned over to them. In fact anything that their parents owned, should the children happen to fancy it, was at once put at their command. Oh, those Southern parents! Those wonderful, incredible, absurd, divine parents—with never a night to call their own and never a thought but that it's a blessed privilege to be run out of their own living room any night, every night, if only the girls are belles—— Knock on wood!

So the Baker girls had house parties and picnics and friends in for supper. Laura says she can never remember an evening when the place wasn't full of young folks. They played the guitar and the piano, and made lemonade and sandwiches, and danced and gave barbecues, and had twelve for the week end, and the dressmaker in twice a year to sew—only the dresses, though, for their mama made all their exquisite underclothes herself by hand, yards and yards of hand-embroidered ruffles for their petticoats, miles of rolling and whipping and hemstitching on their nighties and wrappers and corset covers. In case the very young require a translation here, let me explain that a wrapper was a negligee and a corset cover was the sort of bra that made the tenderest and most supple girl look more like a good firm upholsterer's job than a human being.

When everything was ready, pleated, gored, tucked, crisped and made fragrant, it was packed up, the girls given their railroad fare and dispatched on those long, leisurely visits that were part and parcel of Southern life in that day . . . and, on one of these, Laura hit Paducah as the guest of the Thornbury girls, with whom she had roomed at Belmont College in Nashville.

Paducah was what you might call a severe jolt to her. And the oldest Cobb boy, Irvin, chief jolter. Remember, she was the girl who had but recently suffered a public humiliation because of so far forgetting herself as to laugh out loud in a public place, and picture her shocked horror when she found herself stepping off the train in a strange town, and being welcomed by a select contingent of the town sports, who had not only hired the instruments of the local brass band with which to make loud acknowledgment of her presence, but had provided an open carriage in which to ensconce her and her hostesses, and having draped same with banners, then escorted it, and them, through the open streets, in close formation if not close harmony. The boy who led the parade, and beat on the big drum, loudly but not in time, with his socks falling down over his shoes and his face full of chewing gum, was Irvin.

That morning the *jeunesse dorée* of Paducah, Kentucky, managed to cause two runaways and to implant in the heart of their honored guest a passionate resolution to get out of this crude and dreadful place, and away from these awful boys, just as soon as the next train left for the Deep South. If not sooner.

That night, according to the custom of the country, all the boys came to call at the Thornburys' house. And Laura postponed her departure—after all, she could flit tomorrow . . . or even the day after. Of course one had never met any boys quite like these, and of course Savannah wouldn't approve of them, but . . .

But they were the funniest, the most vital, the most alive people she had ever met in all her life. She says, to this day, that there was never anyone like them.

So she was fascinated, in spite of herself. And why not? Was she not encountering the gusto, the vigor and the laughter of the frontier, still inherent in the children of those who had once sought the far horizon, and pioneered in the "Dark and Bloody Land"?

So she succumbed. She decided to like them all. Except Irvin. Vitality or no vitality, funny or not funny, she thought he was awful. And she would *not* laugh at him. He nearly broke her down once, when the other boys were teasing him about his brand-new mustache, which was very young and soft, and mysteriously pink of hue, and he said, "Now, fellows . . . is it fair to jump on something when it's *down?*"

She had to bite her lip. But no! She would *not* laugh at him. She would die before she would laugh at him. Or notice him. Or encourage him. Or marry him.

So after two years she jilted the beau that she had always planned to marry someday, and because Irvin was still trying to make her laugh, and though sometimes succeeding, most usually not, she married him.

At least that's the best explanation that can be got out of her nowadays. She grows very coy and confused when pressed on this subject, and babbles a lot about the other beau, and how attractive he was, and what a sweet person, and then she sighs and says, "Dear Harry! But then that was before I got engaged to your father."

"But that's what I want to know. Why did you get engaged to my father?"

"I can't seem to remember. He wanted me to be."

My guess is that she was in love with him.

This is what he wrote about his marriage.

When we stood up before the minister and I repeated after him the words, "with all my worldly goods I thee endow," I could not help grinning inwardly. All my worldly goods, as nearly as I could recall at the moment, consisted of two suits of clothes, a set of Ridpath's *History of the World,* and a collection of postage stamps. My salary was eighteen dollars a week.

In those days eighteen dollars a week, in a small town in the Middle West, wasn't affluence but it wasn't starvation either. In fact they could have got on darned well . . . if they had had it. But this princely sum was not all theirs for the squandering. There was the family. He had only been supporting them since he was fourteen. He was twenty-three now. Why, mercy, you couldn't expect them to get anything much arranged in only nine years, now could you?

Years and years afterward my father, with the bitterest, hurt, lost, young look on his face, told me that he thought his mother never forgave him for getting married, for in so doing he was failing in his bounden duty to give everything he could make to his sisters and to her. So here was a merry welcome for a bride. She was the interloper. She was the woman taking their bread out of their mouths. And she had literally to do that, three meals a day, because although she and Dad did set up a little apartment of their own, they paid for and ate their meals at his mother's, so that the rest of the troop would not go hungry.

Laura had known that this must be so, if all were to live, and personally I think she was a pretty game girl to face it. But she had no idea what a strange, strong and complex family she was entering, and she had no idea of how to go about

making them her friends and breaking down their fantastic—
or what seemed to her fantastic—resentment of her.

My father adored his mother. The tragedy of his life was
that he thought that she did not care for him. He has told me
that she had but one child—her eldest daughter Reubie. Reubie!
Something went awfully wrong for her! She was a tiny
woman with wonderful red hair, a face so piquant that it
could be really lovely at times, and was always attractive. Add
to this the figure of a pocket Venus, Cinderella's feet (size one
and a half triple A at the age of sixty), the ankles of a fairy
princess. Here was a girl as witty, and as bitter, as a female
Jonathan Swift, a girl in a million, a girl capable of anything.
But something had happened to her when she was very young
—what I think no human being ever knew, perhaps not even
her own mother—but whatever it was, from that minute she
shut herself in the house, drew the blinds, and only peered
from behind them all day long, to spy upon and mock
and laugh at her neighbors—especially those with big feet—and
not only cut herself off from all her own friends but managed to close the house so that the friends of her brothers and
sister came there not at all. Do young girls still do this? Is the
salt of the earth still spilled out, and lost, like this?

For her this life continued for years. And then she got engaged to a charming and prominent man. They were engaged
for forty years. Forty years! Every night of her life he came
by for her after supper and they went for a ride in the country.
The rest of her life changed not at all. Even in the days when
she was shut away from life entirely, she had been most fastidious and "stylish." Now she took hours to dress for that nightly
ride. It was not until she was well past middle age that the
house was open to visitors. And three days after her mother
died, when Reubie was in her sixties, she was married to her
old beau. They neither of them lived a year.

I think, myself, that my grandmother dedicated herself to the crippled child—and what was Reubie but a crippled child? —but that didn't make things any happier for the rest of her offspring. My Aunt Manie, Dad's younger sister, shudders at the memory of her childhood in that shuttered, black house. I think that it was not possible for anyone to hate a person more than my father did his sister Reubie, when he and she were young. In the last few years of his life he grew very fond of her. Why? (A) She, at last, had learned to appreciate his quality. (B) She did a magnificent job of looking after his mother. She nursed, cooked, cosseted, worked like a Trojan, laughed all the time, was always funny, and dainty as a rose tree. Besides amusing him very much, she looked delightful, hung out the big welcome banner whenever he came home, cooked or planned the cooking of all the things he liked best to eat, made him feel cock of the walk. It is very hard to stay angry with a woman who makes you laugh, and feeds you.

But that was a long, long time in the future, and not to be foreseen on the day when young Irvin and young Laura first came to board with the family.

They had been married at her house in Savannah and it was a lovely wedding. They had a beguiling custom in the friendly South of that day of sharing *all* the fun of the party—that is, the preparations as well as the results. Your best friends and neighbors would gather at your house and help make the sandwiches and fix the flowers, and then these nice people would all go home, dress up, come back, and say how good the food was and how pretty everything looked.

That's the way it was at their wedding: the best man made the great bell of sweet peas that hung over the table, and the bridesmaids wove the ropes of smilax, and all the uncles came to help mix, or at least sample, the punch. Oh, that punch! It is a guarded and cherished secret of the Chatham Artillery, an

organization into which most of the members are born, like
Groton or Mohammedanism, but even the uninitiates can get
beautifully potted on their celestial tipple.

My grandfather Baker presented me with the recipe, with
the suggestion that I serve it at those functions which, he believed, were known as cocktail parties. I thanked him very
much, but have never quite got around to doing same in my
kitchenette apartment. However, if a bunch of Angels, or
Gabriel himself, or any other representatives of the Heavenly
Host ever happen to drop in on me I will try to stir them up a
snort of Chatham Artillery Punch.

This is the recipe for twelve gallons (that's right—gallons), with the penciled note in Granddad's hand that a gallon serves sixteen glasses!

1 pound green tea in 2 gallons water ... allow to stand overnight, then strain. Add

> 3 gallons Catawba, or sweet wine
> 1 gallon St. Croix rum
> 1 gallon Hennessey brandy
> 1 gallon rye whisky
> 5 pounds broken sugar
> 3 quarts maraschino cherries
> Juice of 3 dozen oranges
> Juice of 3 dozen lemons
> 1 gallon Gordon gin

Mix tea and juices first, add sugar and liquids. Let sit in charred oak keg for a week or two (covered). When ready to serve, add ice and *twelve quarts of champagne*.

Do you wonder that the uncles came early?

They hung the house with thousands of sweet peas and all the bridesmaids carried shower bouquets of the same flowers, so that forever after Irvin was highly sentimental about sweet peas, although quite incapable of recognizing them when growing upon a vine in a garden. He sent my mother a bunch of them on every anniversary, and twice, to my knowledge, this laudable and husbandly act caused near disasters.

Once the anniversary came around at a time when he had just quit the newspaper business to free-lance as a short-story writer and was living on his capital, and this, never what one might call a lordly sum, had dwindled until it would hardly serve as a nest egg for a church mouse. Still and all, sweet peas were a "must" for the twelfth of June, so he gave me, aged seven, a twenty-dollar bill and told me to stop on my way home from school and order my mother her bouquet. He meant to blow about a dollar and a half or so on the floral tribute, but either he did not make himself clear, or I was swept away with the excitement of having all that money to spend, for spend it all I did.

Our house was mighty pretty, if a little overperfumed, for the next few days, for in those simple days for twenty bucks you could buy enough sweet peas to festoon the Grand Central Station, but they do tell me we ate as little and as seldom as possible for quite a while afterward. Certainly the flowers were faded and gone before we could have company for dinner again.

The other time Dad's thoughtfulness concerning anniversaries caused what might be called A CATASTROPHE IN SWEET PEAS was when my mother was visiting her mother down at Tybee Beach, that little silver and blue slice of sea sand and oleanders off Savannah. My Aunt Betty and her husband, Uncle Harry, were also guests there at the time, and an old school friend was coming down for the day. When Laura woke up that morning her mother, whom we all called Mama, was standing at the foot of the bed with her arms full of the gay flowers, and she, usually the merriest and sweetest of women, was weeping, not hard but steadily, and as one not to be comforted.

"Here," said Mama, "are your flowers from that wonderful Irvin! He w-w-w-wired to your father to order them."

Upon which she cast them to the ground and let the full force of the gathered storm come a-gushing.

"What in the world is the matter with *you?*" demanded my mother.

"It's your father," sobbed Mama. "I've been married to him for thirty years and he n-n-n-never sent me a f-f-f-lower." And she fled, sobbing aloud, to lock herself in her room. My grandfather tried to lure her out with much sweet talk, but when he was answered first by a stony silence, and then with low murmurs to the effect that he was a brute who did not love her, he dashed out of the house roaring, to anyone interested, that he had dedicated his life to that woman, and because he hadn't spent three dollars on a miserable little bunch of flowers she had turned on him in his old age and was bringing his gray hairs in sorrow to the grave. And they could expect him back when they saw him.

"Well," said my Uncle Harry, "I must say your mother is being very unjust to Papa Baker."

"Is that so?" said my Aunt Betty, rising from the table, and emitting from her person such smoke and flame that both by night and by day she could have served as a guide in the desert to the Hebrew children. "I think that my father has been very cruel to my mother.... And you are no better! Ten years ... ten long years, I have been married to *you* ... and have I ever had a flower?" And she, too, burst into tears, and fled to her room. The house was beginning to look, and smell, that damp and salty it might have been high tide during the hurricane season!

My Uncle Harry, being a tougher character than my grandpapa, wasted no time in cajolery, but cast his breakfast to the floor, announcing in a voice that could be heard without amplifiers for several miles that though it was true he had not sent flowers on his last anniversary, it was also true that he had bought his wife a new Stanley-Steamer automobile which might have made up for the omission. And if anyone was interested, they could expect *him* when they saw him.

On his way down to the station he passed Jenny, the expected guest, coming from the early-morning train, and she fairly flew the rest of the way to ask what in the world was the matter with Harry? Laura explained, adding that she thought her mother and Betty were behaving very badly in-

deed, whereupon Jenny, in her turn, hearing why, began to
sniffle and in a voice modulated by gulps said that as a woman
contemplating divorce, *she* understood them only too well, and
. . . Well, by the time Laura had ministered to three separate
sets of hysterics she was a little overwrought her own self, and
marched down to the telegraph office, meaning to warn my
father that from now on she thought it inadvisable to notice
any anniversaries which might occur while she was staying in
this house, but was so upset that she worded her message badly
and sent him something like this: NEVER DARE SEND ANY MORE
FLOWERS TO ME HERE.

Dad didn't speak to her with anything remotely resembling
affection for some weeks.

But all this was long in the future when the bride and groom
got on the train to go to Washington, D. C., in June, for their
honeymoon. Washington in June! The poor innocents! They
arrived late in the evening and it was as hot as—it was as hot
as Washington in June!

Dad suggested that they have supper in their room and
(the sophisticated old *bon vivant!*) ordered stuffed tomatoes
and a bottle of champagne. This, he told Laura, would make
her forget how tired and hot she was. He was perfectly right.
She tasted her first glass dubiously, but then cried: "Why, this
is better than any lemonade I ever had in my life! I don't want
this little old glass—I want a tumblerful!"

Dad said she made a world's record that night and, moreover, one that so far as he knew has never been equaled, much
less bettered, for she passed out cold as a herring in something
under five minutes, scaring the living daylights out of him. He
sent for the hotel doctor and in distracted tones informed him
that his bride was dead. "Dead, my foot!" said this callous
character. "She's drunk as hell!"

"Well," said Dad, "there is one thing about my present

wife—she's certainly an inexpensive little thing. One hot dog, and she's sick. Ten cents' worth of beer and she's high as a kite! She couldn't blow two bits on a wild party to save her life!"

When the honeymoon was over they went first to Louisville for a while and then back to Paducah. Irvin had been the youngest managing editor of a daily paper in the United States at one time, but he was almost twenty-four now and an old stager.

They fixed up their little flat (they had a rubber plant and lots of cut glass and silver—wedding-present loot, of course) and began to board with the family, and he went back to work. Lordy! Lordy! how he did work! In a book called *Stickfuls* which was his first try at autobiography, he has written the story of how and why he became a newspaperman, and when the excerpts from that book which follow here are read they make it all sound mighty colorful and funny and fine, a life that any sixteen-year-old boy might envy.

What I needed was a job that had an immediate pecuniary connection to it. So I scouted round town, and I was just about to land a place in the city passenger office of one of the two railroads, at three dollars a week to start on, when one night my father came home and asked me how I would like to be a newspaperman.

It did not take more than a second to make up my mind. . . . To be a regular newspaper reporter, with a pad of paper and a pencil in my pocket, going round gathering news items and writing them out to be read, struck me as a much more dignified and important calling than running errands for a railroad company. Besides, I had felt all along that I was not cut out for a commercial career. I had never learned the multiplication table—and never have yet. . . .

Even [very] far back I had felt that writing was my proper trade. . . . My earliest known photograph shows me, at the

tender age of twenty months, lying flat upon my stomach—I
could lie flat upon my stomach then—engaged in scribbling
upon a sheet of paper with a stub of pencil. Tradition has it
that on this occasion, having been dressed in my Sunday best
and taken under parental escort to the photographer's establishment, I resolutely refused to be interested in the promise
of the officiating functionary that a little bird was about to
come out of the black box. It would seem that at that moment,
I cared little for ornithological phenomena. It is also recorded
that I howled, opening my mouth widely. . . . I must have
looked a good deal like a detachable rim. Now, my parents
did not desire to have an interior view of me. They knew already that I possessed superior acoustic qualities, and had no
wish to preserve the revealed aspects of my personal sounding-
board. . . . Rather, they longed that I might be shown with
my features composed; for already the Home Beautiful movement was sweeping through America. . . .

I have been told that I wept unabatedly and whole-souledly,
until my mother . . . put into my fingers a scrap of lead-pencil.
Immediately I became calm, and a faded photograph which is
now treasured in the family archives was a result. . . .

So when my father made the suggestion to me that I might
get a job on [a] paper . . . I jumped at the prospect . . . [and]
the next morning at eight o'clock—the date was January six-
teenth—I went to work as a newspaper reporter . . . experience
has taught me that there never was and never will be a newspaper office just like the one in which I made my start.

The principal owner was one of the most lovable men that
ever lived. Mainly he presided over the business department.
When a farmer came in and paid his subscription for the
weekly edition—which was two dollars by the year—Boss Jim,
as everybody called him, would pitch one dollar into the cash
drawer; and then, without a word, he would make for the door.
All within sight who could spare the time—bookkeepers, reporters, pressmen, printers, loafers—would trail after him as he
led the way to Uncle John's place next door; and there they
would line up in a row at the bar while Boss Jim spent the

dollar on toddies at ten cents apiece. Sometimes this would happen half a dozen times a day. . . .

If they had only one reporter they had editors to spare. There was a river editor, who handled the steamboat column. . . . There was an exchange editor, a mentally alert but physically indolent man who seemed to live entirely on chewing tobacco and clippings. There was an editorial writer—we were strong on editorials—and there were four elderly men who had a more or less indefinite connection with the paper, writing what pleased them when it pleased them. . . . Three of these were Confederate veterans, and the fourth was a Union veteran, who had drifted in from somewhere up North years before and, finding the climate congenial and the whisky at Uncle John's place unexcelled, had remained ever since—shabby, scholarly, irresponsible, a gentleman drunk or sober—the first real newspaper Bohemian, and the only real one I ever saw. He wrote only when the spirit moved him; but he could write like a house afire. I remember well the day they fished his body out of the river. The theory always was that, being overtaken with fatigue, he went to sleep on the deck of the wharfboat and walked in his sleep. . . .

It was into this unique establishment that I was welcomed of a brisk January morning. . . . The editor finished whatever he was doing, and then he opened a drawer and gave me one of those old-fashioned red-cedar pencils with a vein of slate running through its center. He offered me a pad of paper too, but I was already provided in that direction . . . and then he told me to go out and try to find some items. I remember my bewildered feeling as I buttoned my overcoat round me and stepped out into the wind-blown street. Always before this street had seemed to me fairly to throb with life and movement. Now, all of a sudden, it had become as cold and empty as an open grave. It looked as if nothing had ever happened there; as if nothing ever was going to happen there.

I wandered round in a lost sort of way until I came to the Market Square, where a few hucksters shivered at their stalls under the long open shed. There I got my first item [and] . . .

thanks to a sort of photographic gift of mind which has been my best asset as a reporter, I can still see this my first item just as it appeared in the paper that evening. . . . "Cal Evitts, the efficient and popular market master, says there were more rabbits brought to the local market this week than any week this winter. Molly Cottontails sold this morning for ten cents dressed, or five cents undressed." . . .

For the first three weeks of my apprenticeship nothing was said about pay. It had been understood in a vague kind of way that I would work for nothing until such time as my services became sufficiently valuable to entitle me to wages. At the end of my third week, on Saturday night as I was leaving the office, Boss Jim called me back and pressed some coins into my hand. I could hardly wait to count them. He had given me a dollar and seventy-five cents. Up until then I had felt a haunting uncertainty regarding my real status as a member of the staff, but now all doubt was gone. The proof lay glittering in the palm of my hand. I was a regular newspaper reporter on a regular salary. It is my present recollection that I outgrew a suit of comparatively new clothes over Sunday—the vest especially becoming too tight across the chest.

In two months my pay was four dollars a week and I was writing my share of the paper and more. . . . Seeing how willing to work I was, the principal reporter began letting me cover part of his territory for him. . . . I wrote all sorts of items —court proceedings, trials, crimes, accidents, deaths, notices of the shows that came to the opera house, business changes— even editorial paragraphs of a supposedly humorous nature. I covered the county fair, a big annual event; and I did weddings and political rallies, revival meetings and the opening of new saloons.

At the end of the third year, having been raised to ten dollars a week by then, a wave of mortality hit the paper and overnight Irvin was promoted and had his name stuck up at the top of the editorial page as editor. He wrote:

"I still did plenty of reporting—all country editors do—but I was the editor all the same, and I was only nineteen years old. I was probably the youngest managing editor of a daily paper in the country; undoubtedly I was the worst. I did not have

the judgment or the balance or the experience to fit me for the place; I had only ambition and energy and an ability to throw copy together quickly. And I was as careless and nearly as dangerous as a two-year-old child playing with a box of matches in an oil warehouse.

It was not facts I was after; I only hankered for the details. In a big city I should have been called a faker and yellow. I marvel yet how I got away with it in a small town. But somehow I did! I managed to involve the paper in several good-sized libel suits . . . and I had one or two narrow escapes from being shot by indignant citizens. Down in that country aggrieved persons were not much given to asking damages of a paper that had misrepresented them; they preferred taking it out of the editor's hide. I guess my youth saved me—that and a good stiff bluff on my part. Once or twice I was frightened blue, but I packed a pistol on my hip and talked big and nobody winged me.

Well, that is sort of a Horatio Alger story, isn't it? And it reads mighty lively and spirited, as though the man, writing about the boy who was his young self, remembered it all with humor, and fondly? That is what nostalgia will do, in his case a nostalgia more for the things he did not have than for those he did. At least that is what Laura thinks, and what I think, too. But he never got over being homesick for the food, the speech, the air, the smells, the customs of home. To the last minute of his life he wanted "fried peach pies." "You remember, Loll?" he would ask. "Best things in the world, Mama's fried peach pies." And he wanted turnip greens—cooked with fat meat of course—and corn bread and fried chicken and fried catfish and broiled young quail and biscuits and spoon bread and country sausage and country ham.

A thousand times I've heard him tell the epic tale of the time he and his cousin belled the dog. "A country dog. A feckless, innocent sort of a hound country dog." He always laughed harder at the story than I did, which means he most split his britches, and maybe it wasn't because the story was so terrific, maybe it was because everything connected with the old days seemed to be bigger, and taste better and smell sweeter and, yes, be funnier, than anything ever would be, come nowadays.

Anyhow, one summer morning he had gone out into the country to play with some young cousins of his own age and sex, and along moseyed the country dog. It was one of those listless, steamy days generating lassitude and ennui and when that dog (and they could tell by the look of him, and by the abjectness of his manners, that he wasn't anybody in particular's dog) came sniffing around asking for trouble, just plain begging for trouble really . . . well, they were willing to oblige him. But not immediately, for it was getting on toward lunchtime and Irvin had to go home for that, so they figured on saving up the dog until later in the afternoon when they'd have plenty of time in which to "bell" him and thus liven things up for him a bit, and change his outlook, and give him a new interest in life.

Irvin went home and ate his lunch quick as he could and hurried right back. But one perfidious cousin couldn't wait. He'd gone on ahead and belled the dog all by himself; the "bell" in this case being a tin can tied to the unfortunate's tail. Whereupon the country dog went crazy and started out to run himself to death.

Irvin had just crossed a long, low-walled culvert that led out of town, when he heard the country dog coming. He heard him before he could see him, and you could see him most as far as the eye could reach because of the small, but thick, dust storm he was kicking up and carrying along with him. Irvin, though sore aggrieved that he had not been in on the fun when it started, paused to enjoy as much of the spectacle as possible. He drew back into the bushes, out of the road, to give the country dog room and then . . .

And then there turned in from a side road and onto the culvert, whence it could not possibly retreat nor back up nor pull aside, nor avoid its doom in any way at all, a long, sol-

emn, funeral procession. Not just a regular everyday sort of
funeral, either, for they were burying an old gentleman who
had been what is known as a "joiner." He'd belonged to every
order and organization there was to belong to, so pretty near
the whole town was riding in that funeral, which hit the culvert from one end just as the country dog made it from the
other.

Irvin saw what was coming. Popeyed with horror he slid
into a ditch, and watched. He didn't want to watch, but he
couldn't help himself. There were, he calculated, nineteen
runaways *before* the country dog reached the hearse. The
hearse horses didn't run away. Maybe they couldn't. Maybe all
the place there was to run away in was already occupied. So
they reared instead. Reared and upended the hearse. And the
back door came open and the coffin stood up on end and then
slowly, with a most awful slowness, fell. It first hit the culvert
wall and stood on end again for hours. That's what Irvin says.
Hours. Then the lid came off, the corpse looked the cowering
Irvin right in the eye, and then fell over, and out, and down,
to the dry creek bed below . . . and thereupon it was revealed
to all interested beholders that the corpse was dressed in what
is known as a "half-shroud."

When all was over Irvin did not continue to his cousins'
house. He went home. And in by the back way. And when
suppertime came it seemed that he did not care for any.

Next day he felt some better. Not much, but some, so he
sneaked out to his cousins' house to find out if anything had
happened there. And something indeed had. For his cousins'
father had found out that it was one of his boys who had belled
the dog and broken up the funeral. So he whipped him. In
fact, Irvin's cousin claims that his father whipped him every
time he saw him from then on. He says he came home to see
his father when the old gentleman was eighty, and he getting

on to fifty, and he says his father whipped him the moment he laid eyes on him.

And Irvin claims that he was twenty-five before he ever owned up to his part in it, and past thirty before he thought it was funny.

When he told this story you would have thought, if you judged by his voice, that he had never used any accents except those of the Pennyrile, though in fact the years in New York had changed him so that usually he had but the slightest trace of what is known as a Southern accent.

He suddenly tuned up on us, at about the age of fifty, talking like a Virginian, and a Virginian who had never left home for five split minutes at that. All of a sudden it was "gyarden" and "cyar" instead of garden and car. This brand-new, and very phony talk (for who ever heard a Kentuckian uttering such sounds in his native wood-notes wild?) was received with ribald mockery by his astounded family, but he was impervious, and continued to cultivate his own particular and peculiar dialect, entirely to his own satisfaction. He was just remembering, and remembering wrong, that's all.

And yet this youth after which he thirsted in memory had been so sad. He writes blithely enough of how pleased he was to get that job on the paper, but remember, that job was a necessity and a dire one. And, to make it worse, he had to take it the very year he had thought to be going off to school, as all his cousins and friends went; even his outfit was already ordered, when Dr. Saunders died and there was no one else in the family who was willing or able, or both, to see that this boy got the education after which he thirsted as one in the desert thirsts for water. Naturally, he gave himself one, and a good one, but that is not the point. At least it's not the point to a fourteen-year-old boy who never gets to wear the gaudy new uniform that had been ordered for the military academy, who has to stay at home and watch the other boys go off and—worse, much worse—watch them come home again, privileged characters, with new ways, carefree, irresponsible, concerned with sports and girls and parties and big doings at college, while he was concerned with the rent money and bread and butter, and holding down a job.

Maybe they were just a little condescending to old Irvin who had thus slipped out of their privileged world and become a workingman. At least he thought this; he was forever on the lookout for the condescending note, and if he thought that he detected it, hated the one employing it with an undying hate. An Indian hate, that never forgot, and forgave only for conscience' sake. He was the touchiest man alive and I am sure that there are hundreds of people who have felt the rough end of his tongue—and it could flay—and never knew why it was that when they had approached him with courtesy they suddenly found themselves limping off, held together with bandages.

It was because he was ever on the lookout for a slight, or even the slight that hadn't been dealt him yet, but that he imagined somebody might have stored up on his premises, ready to be dusted off and handed down to Cobb.

It seems to me that most people are funny about the things which they get for themselves and by themselves. Funny in this way: they don't think much of them. What woman likes to tell you she bought her own jewelry, even though she may have earned the money to pay for it by honest, even brilliant work? No, sir! There isn't one of us who isn't proud as Punch if we can put the bite on some soft-headed male, but slightly humiliated at the necessity of spending our own money. Yet it seems to me, in all logic, that the diamond ring that represents one's own achievements should be the one that you brag on. And a man's education is the same. How many self-educated men have I heard say: "I'm self-made . . . and proud of it"? Dozens. How many have I believed when he said this? Not one! But every man jack of them would like to say, "I'm a Harvard, Yale, Oxford, Barber's College man—like my father before me."

Maybe it is because one has to pay one's tuition to the College of Experience with one's heart's blood, which is too precious a medium of exchange; maybe it's because the man or woman who has matriculated there thinks that if his education had been different, life would have been different.

Anyhow, and for whatever reason, Irvin always thought that he had been cheated. And nothing ever made it up to him.

But for a while his sense of loss was poulticed by his love for Laura and hers for him, and indeed, back in Paducah, the young Cobbs had a fine time.

My grandmother—who always prefaced her rare compliments to my mother with these words, "Well, I'll say this much for you, Laura"—once told her, "Well, I'll say this much for you, Laura, you could make a home out of a desert waste, and find friends there before sundown."

So she found friends and he worked. Laura says now that what she remembers most vividly of those days is his coming home from the office, late, late in the night, or more likely, early in the morning, so tired that she could never believe that his tiredness was all that was the matter with him, but, time after time, thought that he was "coming down" with something. He was. With a daily paper that he wrote, edited, put together and all but sold on the streets, single-handed. She always woke up when he came in and then they sat on the foot of the bed and ate supper together. "Oyster loaf," says Laura, with a reminiscent greedy light in her eyes, "and wonderful sandwiches, and the biggest, briniest dill pickles in the world." And he'd tell her the news, and she'd tell him what funny thing the Corbetts had said that day.

Maybe it wasn't *always* the Corbetts, but that's the way it seems now when I'm hearing about it. "As Miss Molly once said to Judge Hal" . . . that's the way Laura begins when she talks about those days.

Judge Corbett was a brilliant man, and the greatest of dears, and Miss Molly, with the face and nature of a merry Madonna, was and is, divinely beautiful, and they had five children who were the town's terrors and the town's darlings, and no money much, ever.

As Miss Molly told me not long ago, when they did get in the chips for a minute or two, something always happened. Prosperity never lingered round their door.

There was the time, for instance, that the Judge made a killing at the Derby. "Next afternoon," says Miss Molly, "Hal bought me a set of Spode china—and that night he lost all the rest of the money at a poker game—and a week or so later Elise was reaching for something on the top shelf and fell on the service plates. But they were very pretty while they lasted."

Once the Judge, mightily in wine, came home very late and, heading for the icebox, found there a beautiful bottle of cold water, of which he drank thirstily, but not greedily, for he nobly left some in the bottle and then went and woke up Miss Molly. "Get up, Molly," he said, "and get all the children up too, and bring them downstairs, right away."

"What in the world is the matter?" demanded Miss Molly in great alarm.

"Nothing, nothing at all," said the Judge. "I just want you to take all the children downstairs right away. . . . I want to give them some of that wonderful water! Why, the poor little things never had anything so good in their whole lives!"

Once the Judge, so Miss Molly tells me, gave her a hundred

dollars with strict orders to buy herself some pretty clothes. "An outfit," he commanded, "head to foot." But Miss Molly thought it over and decided that the "outfit" could wait but the grocery bill couldn't, so, in a decidedly underhanded manner, she up and went and paid it.

That night the Judge arrived home, clamorous to see what Miss Molly had bought herself with the hundred, and was greeted instead by a paid-up grocery bill. "Damn it all, Molly," he roared, "if I'd known that you were going to fool it away, I'd never have given it to you!"

The Corbett wit suffers no diminution with the years, for the latest bit of Corbettiana concerns Ina Claire Langstaff, Miss Molly's granddaughter, who passed the summer of '44 doing the housework in the vast old family home (on account in Paducah the faithful old family retainer is faithfully retaining a war job) and worried herself sick because for a long time she had heard nothing from her fiancé, a young West Pointer, then busy collecting himself some medals and German prisoners in France.

Her father tried to cheer her up. "He probably isn't dead," said he, "but a lot of things can happen to a man when he is far away from home, and in a strange land. . . . Look at your Uncle Tom. . . . He came home from France with a French bride. Your young man is just as liable to turn up with a French bride or an English one—or, for that matter, a Chinese one."

Ina Claire thought this over awhile and then she said, "Well, if she can cook, I'll take them both."

It seems to me, though I may not know what I am talking about, that those who live in small towns are either so deeply part of their own place that they could never be happy in any other, and must, to be happy, be forever rooted to the streets, the faces, the customs, which they have always known; or else they are consumed with a passion to get out into the large world—and spend the rest of their lives trying to make it as much like home as possible. It is a sort of neurosis, the old love-hate stuff—the old one-two.

And Laura and Irvin were different about this, as they were about so many things. Because he was in love with his town, and she was in love with New York, which she had seen just once. Left to his own devices, I think that he would have stayed "back home"; left to hers, I don't think she would have stayed in *any* small town for as much as a long week end. So I guess she started working on him just about right away.

"Don't be an idiot, Loll," he said. "What can I do in New York? I'm fine here . . . but there are a million like me in that town."

"There isn't *anyone* like you, *anywhere,*" said she, and though she did not make him believe it, not quite, she made him go.

It took a while though . . . three years. And part of that time she was too busy with having me, and nursing me, to bother much about anything except staying alive herself, and then seeing that I followed her example. And that was a business! It makes a Homeric tale: the midnight dashes for the doctor, the wild emergency remedies, the weeks when I wouldn't possibly live until Tuesday, and the following week when I couldn't possibly live until Wednesday. Poor, young, driven things! With the doctor's bills piling up, and the baby never getting any better. The baby crying . . . crying. . . .

I would not sleep unless I could sleep on my mother's stomach, and I would not condescend to settle down there unless first my father walked me for hours. "A million miles," he said with considerable feeling, "a million miles I toted you, while you yelled your fool head off."

He carried me over one shoulder, and keeping me "planté

là," with one hand, used the other to hold and turn the book he was trying to read as he wearily trudged up the dawn. It was a big expensive book, and he had saved and scrimped a long time before he could buy it. It was called *American Birds* and was by Dr. Frank M. Chapman. This was a coincidence,

or at least it became one a long time later when I married a bird from the Chapman's nest, *i.e.,* Frank, Jr. That was a fine wedding and I don't suppose my father, when called upon for a bridal toast, ever found a theme for one so ready-made. Dad did fine with it, too.

Well, they got me born and about two years old and then they could begin to think about the big move again. It seemed an impossibility. They had a baby. He had no job to go to. They didn't have any money at all. His mother said that Laura was a wicked woman who was trying to take her son away from her. And perhaps in the deepest sense of the word this was true, as it is always true when the terrible conflicts between mother and wife break over the head of the unfortunate, beloved and bedeviled object of their affection.

Irvin went to the big city. Because he wrote a story about a hanging. I've heard him tell the story myself, but the memory always made him a little sick at his stomach, twenty, thirty years afterward. He told me he was gagging all the time he wrote the following account. But for all that it held the fascination of horror for him. He wrote it. He told it many times. It haunted him.

It was while I was editor of the paper that I covered my first hanging. And this hanging linked together my first job with my present one, for the victim was a negro who had worked for my father who at one time had owned an interest in an ice-company. [During one summer vacation, to earn pocket money, I drove one of the wagons while he rode on the back end and handled the ice.] . . . He was a broad, stocky darky, always polite and respectful when dealing with white people, but a black terror among his own race. Now he was about to be hanged for killing a negro woman and I was to write the story of it for my paper. . . .

I spent the night before the hanging at the jailer's house. We played nickel-limit poker until three o'clock in the morning; then we had a fried-fish breakfast, and about an hour before daylight we went to the jail. The condemned man was already up and dressed in a new suit of black clothes. He wore a stiff white collar and a black tie—probably the first collar and the first tie he had ever worn in his life—and his hands were incased in white cotton gloves, and his brand-new shoes had

been given an extra polish by one of the jail trusties. The suit and the shoes were a gift from the sheriff; the white gloves were George's own idea. His name was George, but his own people had a name for him—a tribute to his record. They called him Devil!

This minute I can shut my eyes and see the picture of him as he paced up and down the narrow jail corridor in the half light of the flickery gas-jets. I can see his eight-dollar suit bunching in the back; see his huge gloved hands fluttering like two white pigeons as he chanted snatches of hymns and broken prayers—working himself up to the state of exaltation that sends so many of his race to the gallows shouting-happy. Plastered against the barred cell-doors beyond, like bats, hung ten or a dozen negroes, their eyeballs standing out from the shadowy background like so many pairs of shiny china marbles. In time to the cadence of the Devil they crooned and groaned in a wholly sympathetic half-hysterical chorus. . . .

"Dis time tonight I'll be in glory!" he told them, his voice rising in a long swing, and then sinking low again. "I'll hab a shimmerin' robe upon me an' golden slippahs on my feet. An' I's comin' back to dis yere sinful world to hant de wicked an' de lost!"

From the cells came a long, shivering groan, and through the bars we could see his scared audience shaking in their terror.

"Yes, suh," he went on, "I's comin' back to dis world tonight. An' dat ain't all—I's comin' back to dis yere jail!"

A howl of piteous entreaty arose, so loud that it reached the ears of the negroes gathering in the gloom outside; and they took it up and the whole air everywhere seemed filled with the sounds of their wailings. . . .

The time came to read the death warrant—a needless cruelty imposed by the statutes of our state. There was a hitch here. The sheriff had been made ill by the task ahead of him and was violently nauseated in the jail office. The deputy was outside testing the rope and the trap . . . but the death warrant must be read aloud in the presence of the condemned—the law so provided. Somebody shoved a paper in my hands and I found myself stumbling through the awesome document, while Devil stood facing me with his hands crossed and spread flat upon his breast. He was drinking in the big, impressive words and glorying—visibly glorying—in the importance of his position. And when I was through he thanked me.

"Young Cap'n," he said, giving me my old ice-wagon title, "I always knowed dat ef ever you could do pore old George a favor you suttinly would. Thanky, suh, kindly."

It was after they had tied his hands behind him and had started the march to the scaffold that, for the first time, he showed signs of his distress. His scalp suddenly contorted until a deep V of ridged flesh appeared between his eyes—it was still there when they cut him down.

Hundreds of negro women outside, seeing his head rise above the high fence, set up a dismal quavering song of lamentation; and, as though in defiance of them, a group of reckless young negroes began singing the Devil Song—one of those weird chants that guitar-picking minstrel bards among the Southern negroes write to commemorate a notable crime or a great tragedy. This one dealt with Devil's life and his crime and his trial; and now there were added verses, made up on the spot, to describe his hanging. Just as the drop fell, a negro stretched on the limb of a tree overhanging the inclosure fainted and tumbled off right at our feet. And either the rope was too long—as it so often is—or it stretched under the weight; and poor Devil's feet touched, and he made a long, sickening job of dying.

We assisted in that hanging—another cub-reporter and I. . . . We stood together under the gallows. The agonizing figure of the negro swayed and swung within a yard of us. We saw how the tip of one of his toes was poised exactly upon the peak of a big piece of gravel which lifted above the surface of the jail yard. It sustained his weight—that and the rope about his neck. Something must be done and done quickly else the man would choke by degrees of slow torture; he was making hideous muffled sounds in his throat and twitching and jerking through all of his frame. So one of us caught his bound legs at the bend of the knee and raised them clear and the other kicked the jagged pebble away. His feet did not touch after that although, even so, the margin was so narrow that you could not roll a lead-pencil along the earth beneath him without scraping the soles of his shoes.

Irvin did not think much of the story he wrote about that hanging, and I guess at that he did not write it then as you have read it here. Myself, I think it so wonderfully done that every word gives me the creeps, but just the same he did miss a bet, for he did not collect and write down the words of the Devil Song. He says himself:

I've thought a thousand times since what an opportunity I missed then; but perhaps it's just as well I missed it. Had I

handled the tale differently from the way I did handle it our
subscribers probably would not have cared for it; whereas my
story seemed to give general satisfaction. A number of people
complimented me on it.

Enough people, I guess. Anyhow they seemed to have given
him the last little necessary push. He began to recollect the
boy who had worked on the same paper with him once—for
five dollars a week less—but who was getting sixty-five now in
New York. Sixty-five dollars! If *he* could do it! If that man
could do it, I can do it. Ah, but *can* I do it?

"If that man can make sixty-five, Irvin," said Laura, "*you*
can make a hundred."

He told her not to be so silly, nobody in the world made a
hundred dollars a week, except maybe John D. Rockefeller
and the President, but she did not believe that for a minute.
"When that—that *nobody!*—makes sixty-five, a hundred is
nothing. Not in comparison!"

Then she began writing letters to her father. And that good
man said "Yes." She was to bring the baby home until Irvin
was settled in New York and he would lend the boy two hundred dollars to finance the adventure.

So she packed up and went. They must have been a scared
little sorry couple when he put her on the train. They were
gambling everything they had, and then some. They were pitiful and wonderful. How many thousands like them there have
been and will be, these kids, all the kids, from way back and
from yesterday and of now, all these American kids who have
risked security and loneliness and humiliation and the fear of
real want, to follow the big American dream, the dream of
"getting on"!

Of course they told each other that it would not be for long.
In fact, no time at all, really. For of course he would get a job

right away, and so this was just a chance for her to get a little rest and see the folks, and let them see the baby, who would certainly never be so cute again. And she would write every day, and send him snapshots, if the wonder child changed at all, although of course that would be sort of silly, for you really wouldn't be able to see any change in her; not in the little time she would be away from her daddy.

So good-by—good-by.... Don't be scared.... I'm not scared. Good-by.... *I'm so scared*....

He landed in New York in August. That's how much *those* two knew. They lay off old experienced reporters who have been on a paper for years, in August in New York. It was almost a year before they saw each other again.

Chapter 2

WHEN LITTLE OLD NEW YORK
WAS BAGDAD ON THE SUBWAY

 STARTING this chapter, and fumbling for a lead, an occupational hazard which has driven many a better writer than I to drink, mayhem and excesses of all kinds, at last there came into my head something that I could quote, and if quoting is really petty larceny, why, better a small crime than a big nervous breakdown. I'm not even a very efficient criminal because what I am trying to steal is a line from the *Autobiography* of Feodor Chaliapin and I remember the book but dimly, which by a merciful dispensation of Providence usually is the way one is permitted to remember the autobiographies of singers, these rating, as literature, right along with such works as *My Two Weeks in the Jungle, or How I Did Not Reach Tibet,*" by Colonel Something-hyphen Something, with at least four initials preceding his name and the rest of the alphabet trailing along behind—and a lot snappier reading matter on his calling card than you will ever find in his collected works.

But enough . . . there is no use being morbid, and incidentally I did not set out to pan Chaliapin's book, especially since it is not only very good but, as stated, not remembered very well, although there are critics (and I can name 'em) who wouldn't let a little thing like that slow them up! It was only the word "dimly" that got me off the track. But, to get on

with it, somewhere in Chaliapin's memoirs he falls to talking
of the time when first he went to work (in the salt mines or on
a chain gang or some place equally grim) leaving home so
early in the morning that it was still dark, and coming home
when night had already fallen, so that he never saw the sun
at all. To keep himself from remembering that he was only a
little boy, frightened of the dark roads and very tired, he used
to sing, and it seemed to him that his song would run along
before him and draw him after it.

How beautiful that is! And it seems to me that every boy
who goes forth to prove himself is following just such a song.
When the Sirens sang surely they had more than one tune in
their repertoire, and perhaps this was one and the most seduc-
tive of them all.

Certainly young Irvin was following this music, when,
separated from everybody in the world whom he loved, he
stood on the deck of a ferryboat one summer morning to
watch the big town rise up and smite him with its grandeur.
He says that part of him was scared limp, though he'd have
been parboiled before admitting it, and the other part was full
of glad visions, although he wasn't tipping his hand about
them either, and the emotions coursing through him were that
violent and contradictory that while his brain was whirling
hot his feet were ice-cold, and though his chest was distending
his vest buttons, he had no bones to his knees.

It's a wonder that it was to New York's door he came knocking and not Chicago's. He had had a chance to go to Chicago
several years before, when by a happy accident (happy for him
I mean) two Chicago gangsters (yes, they had them even
then, only they called them crooks) had made a most daring
and audacious escape from an Illinois jail and an outraged con-
stabulary, who instantly began to catch hell from the newspapers. The men, heading south, were captured at last by a

country sheriff in a tiny town near Paducah. Dad had been making a little extra now and then by acting as local correspondent for a Chicago paper, so, sniffing big money—say as much as ten dollars even—he dropped all and high-tailed it out to the country quick as he could. The escape had been a big story in Chicago, for one of the men, Christopher Merry, was a notorious person and the police offered a handsome reward, while the papers, to chivvy the cops, augmented this sum, the result being that half the towns in the Middle West had laid violent and excited hands upon the wanted men . . . only it always turned out that those safe in custody were only a couple of abashed and apologetic tramps and not the murdering, dangerous and valuable ruffians. For weeks at each false alarm the Chicago papers had sent contingents of experienced reporters to every little town with a couple of hooligans in its jail and high expectancy of reward money in its heart, and they were getting quite considerably fed up with the whole business. So when this last excited claim came in they simply did not bother to investigate, and Irvin got the whole, big, fat, juicy story all to his lone self. The only trouble was that he didn't know what to do with it now that he had it, and having sent one short and colorless paragraph over the wires was about to sign off, when the answer came back:

"SOUNDS LIKE A BIG STORY. WRITE IT FULLY."

He writes of this night:

I had already written in bulletin form . . . the narrative of the escape and the flight [and] now altogether reckless of consequences and filled with the unapproachable joy of creation and authorship, turned myself loose on what I conceived to be a thrilling picture of that pair of trapped ruffians, sitting with their chained ankles in that little box of a jail, bragging how they had outwitted the whole Chicago police department. I always liked to do descriptive stuff, anyhow, whereas a recital of plain facts hampered my style and circumscribed my fancy.

Just the same, midway, and in full flight, he was suddenly scared spitless by the magnitude of the telegraph bill he was piling up. What if they suddenly came to their senses, back there in Chicago, and decided that they did not want all this stuff after all? So he wired, with his heart in his mouth, asking if they were sure, and the answer came back instantly:

LET IT ALL COME. SPREAD YOURSELF AND KEEP SENDING UNTIL WE SAY STOP.

Says he:

I spread myself all right. I wrote and I wrote and I wrote. . . . It was nearly two o'clock in the morning—Sunday morning—before they finally shut off my flow of literature. The message read:

THAT'S ENOUGH. GOOD STUFF! GOOD BOY! GOOD NIGHT!

. . . On Monday morning I got a letter postmarked Chicago, and I opened the envelope to find inside a single sheet of notepaper bearing the heading: Editorial Rooms, the *Tribune*. The following lines were written on it in a somewhat crabbed hand:

"*Dear Sir:* You did excellent work in covering the Merry story for this paper, and I wish to thank you.

"I have instructed the cashier to send you a check for fifty dollars as a bonus.

"Yours truly,

"JOSEPH MEDILL."

I was tickled naturally to get such a letter—particularly was I tickled by the second paragraph—but in the abysmal depths of my fathomless ignorance I attached no particular importance to the fact that Joseph Medill himself had written, with his own hand, to express his appreciation of what a stranger had done for his paper. I knew that the editor or the publisher of the *Tribune* was a man named Medill, but in my conceived estimates the only really great and conspicuous editors of America were Henry Watterson, Henry W. Grady and Murat Halstead, in the order named. A Medill more or less meant nothing to me.

So he spent the money (he was courting Laura then so she got her share of it in the form of a large heart-shaped box of chocolates) and carried the letter around for a day or so, and then forgot all about it, and so missed his chance, maybe, to work under the editor who in later years he came to think the greatest of them all. But when there began all the big talk about the big move he remembered that letter again, and so for a while held out for an attempt at landing a job in Chicago, where somebody or other just might happen to remember the story that he had done for the *Tribune,* whereas in New York there wasn't a soul who had ever heard of him; at least not a soul who could give him a job.

But Laura asked, "Isn't New York the mecca of all news-papermen?"

"Well, yes, but . . ."

"Isn't New York bigger than Chicago?"

"Yes, but you see, Loll . . ."

"We're going to New York," said Laura.

So there he was, standing on the ferry.

He had in his pocket the address of a boardinghouse on West Fifty-seventh Street, along with a batch of letters of introduction; and before the first night had passed he was already lonely, and after two days knew that his letters weren't going to get him anywhere at all, though for two weeks he kept on presenting them, and for two weeks never got by the office boy. Not once. He did see the man whose example had helped him decide on coming east, and who had written him that it would be no trouble at all, but a pleasure, to find an opening for him, only to learn the distressing truth that if said friend found an opening anywhere he'd want it for himself.

Then as a last resort he looked up another acquaintance, a man whom he had known years before down south. This person was now holding down a copyreading job on a second-rate paper. Irvin sent his card in and the man did come out to greet him, but with studied reserve. However when he found that Irvin was *not* trying to borrow money he warmed slightly —not much, but some—enough anyhow to listen to the story.

"My God, man!" he said. "Do you mean to say you gave up a good job as editor of a country paper, where you were your own boss, to come up here and try to break into one of these madhouses? Say . . . that job you quit isn't still open, is it? . . . Because if it is I could get down to Kentucky myself, by day after tomorrow."

There went by two weeks, of heat, of weariness, for he was canvassing every paper in town every day, and mostly on foot to save carfare, of increasing desperate loneliness and with panic growing in him every minute, and his money running lower than a California river in the dry season.

One hot noontime he found himself on a bench in Madison Park, tired and more discouraged than that. It didn't help any to consider the woefully bleak, hopeless faces of his neighbors on the near-by benches, nor to remember that Loll would be worrying herself sick by this time. He'd been writing her the most optimistic and glowing letters, brilliant little works of fiction, and appreciated by her as such. But she knew all right! He could write the funniest letter in the world, and not get any real mirth out of the girl unless somewhere tucked away among the gags was the news that he had a job. And no kidding!

Then he had an inspiration. He said that it was the only

genuine simon-pure inspiration he ever did have, and he knew
that it came from on high because it worked and, what's more,
it always worked, though he utilized it only twice, that day
and again years later when he was in Belgium as a war correspondent and had the whole German Army mad at him—or
at least all that part of the German Army which he had thus
far encountered—and although two successes may not seem
sufficient to brag on, it seems that successes gained thus are
different, inspirations being chancy by nature and frail withal,
neither standing up well in the cold light of reason nor in

results achieved, so if a pay-off in inspiration is rare, two pay-offs are a miracle and may be claimed as such.

This one lifted him off the park bench as if he had been bee-stung. In half an hour he was in his hall bedroom composing a form letter. It wasn't a very long letter but in it he tried to pile a heaping measure of that flippant tone that seemed so popular in the New York papers.

He wound it up, as he recalled, something like this:

This is positively your last chance. I have grown weary of studying the wall-paper design in your anteroom. A modest appreciation of my own worth forbids me doing business with your head office boy any longer. Unless you grab me right away I will go elsewhere and leave your paper flat on its back right here in the middle of a hard summer, and your whole life hereafter will be one vast surging regret. The line forms on the left; applications considered in the order in which they are received; triflers and professional flirts save stamps. Write, wire or call at the above address.

Then he went out and bought a supply of the handsomest paper he could find, gilt-edged and cream-laid, and finding a hotel stenographer had her make thirteen separate copies—not carbon copies—addressing each one to a different managing editor. She said he was the biggest nut she had ever met in her life, but between giggles she managed to make the copies. He dropped them in a letter box and went home feeling highly satisfied with himself and his day's work. He had a feeling that a job was on its way. It was.

The next morning he got up early and for his first call chose the office of the *Sun,* because it seemed to him the best written and best edited of them all. He sent in his card to the managing editor, for the twelfth or thirteenth time. Only this time the response was different for the editor came clear out of his office holding his copy of the letter in his hand.

"Are you the same man who wrote this damn-fool letter?"
he asked. Irvin admitted it.

"Well!" he said, "if you have half as much ability as you
have gall, consider yourself hired."

"All right," said Irvin. "I'm hired."

He started work the next morning—at fifteen dollars a week.
And that night when he got home he found that five other
managing editors, including Arthur Brisbane, were willing to
give him a chance on the strength of that sassy letter.

Now the significant part of the story is that it *was* a nervy
thing to do; it did take a lot of gall. And he didn't have any.
He was just pretending as hard as he could. That touchy man,
that shy man, was doing actual violence to his own nature
when he forced himself to "sell" himself. The only way, in
this world, that he could ever have pulled that bluff was on
paper. If he had attempted it in person—say, by sending in his
card with some flippant message on it—and having been admitted then met with a rebuff, he might very likely have
socked the rebuffer on the nose, but he would never have stuck
around and pestered him until he got a job.

I know that this is so, for I remember him telling me, ruefully enough, of his one attempt at becoming a salesman. Back
in Paducah, an old friend had once come to him with the
proposition that he quit the newspaper, where he was both
overworked and underpaid, and start in selling insurance, a
profession which looked as though it might offer a bright
future to a boy who knew everybody in the county, was a
good mixer, and could make a bronze buddha laugh out loud.

Irvin demurred, there being no native ardor for the insurance business burning in his young breast, but his friend bullied
him into an attempt.

"Look," he said: "we'll make your first sale an easy one. In
fact this sale is already as good as consummated. There is an

old man out in the country . . . I've been working on him a long time and he's just sent word that he's ready to sign. All you have to do is take the papers out to him on Sunday afternoon, get his signature and drive home again. What's more, he fought in Bob Cobb's command and he'll be tickled to death to see you. There's nothing very hard about that, now, is there?"

So Irvin hired a horse and buggy and drove out the following Sunday. He started in pretty good heart but as he jogged along by himself he grew unhappier and unhappier, and less and less self-confident, and would have turned back half a dozen times if he hadn't been firm, not to say relentless, with himself.

But when he arrived, he was received warmly as advertised, being Colonel Bob's kin, and hospitably urged to draw up a chair and make himself at home.

He and his host ensconced themselves on the front porch. At first they got along fine, chatting away about the Colonel and the war and politics, but after they had exhausted each other's opinions on these matters the conversation grew less and less vivacious until finally they fell to discussing the crops, of which Irvin knew little, and the weather, which topic, as they were in agreement that it was unseasonably hot, offered but little scope for animated discourse.

Finally, in pure desperation, they began on Colonel Bob all over again.

Dad says that then his host began to take on a curious resemblance to a stuffed moose head: a resemblance not at all apparent until now. Perhaps it came from the glazed eye he had got on him suddenly, and a queer lengthening of his upper lip and the really alarming distention of his nostrils.

As for Dad, if provided with a suitable weapon, he would almost certainly have committed suicide.

The evening shadows grew long, and still they struggled on with this ghastly conversation, and still Irvin was quite unable to introduce the subject of insurance, and so get the signature and say good-by and go home, nor yet could he bring himself to admit defeat, give in, and up, and go home anyhow.

Finally the old gentleman, as one who abandons all hope, asked Irvin if he wouldn't stay for supper. By this time Irvin was as near idiot as a normal person could be, but the protective instinct came to his rescue, so he managed to refuse, and gulping a miserable cowardly gulp, said, well, he guessed he'd better be getting on now.

He went slowly down the steps, and the light was returning into his host's eyes, and at the last possible moment Irvin turned back, and the light went out again.

"Look here," said Irvin. "You don't really want any insurance, do you?"

"Well," said his host, "now that you put it like that, I'm not sure that I do."

"That's what I thought," said Irvin, and fled.

The next day the old man drove into town to tell Dad's friend that he had definitely changed his mind about taking out insurance, the half-witted Cobb boy having put him off the notion somehow.

So it was a grand thing for him that his letter worked. As he walked out of the *Sun* office that morning, jubilant were his feet. First thing he wired Laura—although not telling her the size of his salary, preferring to break that blow in a letter.

Then he settled down to learn how to be a big-town newspaperman, which is a whole lot different from running a one-man country paper.

It didn't seem to him that he got ahead very fast, although five dollars by five dollars his pay crawled up to thirty a week,

half of which he sent home. Plenty of times he was sore at
heart and discouraged—for it seemed that he never would be
able to get anything distinctive into the paper—and all the time
he was most desperately lonely. He had no friends and no
money. He says that he looked, and looked in vain, for the
Bohemian newspaperman who, he had been led to suppose,
was so common a type in New York. "That carefree, reckless,
gifted, irresponsible, dashing race, who regularly fraternized
together over mugs of musty ale in fascinating little dram-
shops."

Real newspapermen, he says, are never Bohemians, and
despise men who pose as Bohemians. "They are mainly hard-
working, steady-paced persons, with families to support; and
when they get through work they go home to their families
and stay there."

What he means is—that is what he did. I know! He may
not have dug up any carefree, reckless, gifted, irresponsible
and dashing pals for himself, but later on I provided him with
liberal quantities of such characters, and let me tell you that
was a big mistake all round, and for all hands. His reception
of them varied from awful to awfuller to awfullest. If he was
in a bad humor, he would fix any gifted irresponsible with an
eye to quell dragons and snarl slightly. If he happened to be
feeling affable he would ask them if they worked steady and
how was it their wives and children didn't happen to be along
today, or if not provided with these accessories, why not? Also
he knew (heaven knows he knew!) that writing was hard
labor, and he might have conceded that painting could pretty
well use up a man's time and energy, but I am quite sure that
he never got it through his head that musicians might occasionally have to work a little too. In his heart of hearts he
probably thought Arturo Toscanini a common loafer. So if
any of these gay, mad types, whom he says that he yearned to

know, happened to be musical then he *knew* they were skulkers of the first order. And the back of his hand, and the sole of his foot, to them!

One of the things I learned from him is that it is very unwise to judge a man by his profession. *All* writers, in the popular imagination, are gay Bohemian dogs, wasteful, improvident dreamers. Oh, yeah? . . . If that is a description of Irvin Cobb, then Herbert Hoover is a golden-hearted troubadour and Henry Ford a master of madcap mirth!

He lived, worked, thought, and conducted his affairs exactly like any other conscientious middle-class citizen. . . . No . . . he never would have been really happy in any "fascinating little dramshop." Also, as there was never a time in his entire life when he didn't want to go to bed by ten-thirty at the latest, any mad revels were going to have to get rolling a lot earlier than is customary for such affairs—that is, if he were to be among those present—much earlier . . . six-fifteen at the latest, I'd say.

Now this was the year 1904, and although, to the very young, it may seem that I am talking about days before the writ of history runs, I assure them that by then we had got out of the ice age and were beginning to work in copper. It was quite a little place, New York! O. Henry was alive and writing tales about Bagdad on the Subway, although it wouldn't be long now before he was to turn on his deathbed to ask Bob Davis if the sun had come up yet, and on being told no, that it was still some hours to dawn, and sigh and say, "That's too bad! You see, I'm afraid to go home in the dark." I never knew whether he was quoting a popular song or inventing one with his last breath.

Pretty girls wore high collars and buttoned boots and violets and tried their very best to conform to the aesthetic prejudices of Charles Dana Gibson. At Martin's you got the best French cooking, at Jack's the best Welsh rabbit. DeWolf Hopper and Fred Stone and Willy Collier were making the town laugh and Richard Harding Davis was the best-looking man in the world and writing the most enchanting stories.

That Davis! I guess you might call him the male Clare Boothe Luce of his day. Smart and pretty too! And his Van Bibber was still the lovely young man with the gentle heart and the inherited income and the fur-lined overcoat, who took rides in the park, and rescued young lovers from a fate worse than death (that being a wedding without an officiating bishop and some of the Right Names present, and registered as so being in the social column of the *Times*).

Van Bibber the darling! Later on he came to a sad end. You see he grew old and rich and started going to Newport for the summer. And there only a couple of years ago he sat next to a friend of mine at dinner and began, of course, a long harangue against "that man in the White House." She, thinking that in his overexcited condition he might do his aged self some violence tried to calm him by telling him that she too had voted against Franklin Roosevelt, upon which he turned upon her shouting, "Franklin Roosevelt? What are you talking about? Franklin Roosevelt indeed! I'm referring to Theodore!"

But Irvin did not know any of these folks. On fifteen a week one does not do much mingling with the mighty. He did meet Mark Twain, being sent to interview him and finding him a cross old man in a room stained and evil-smelling from tobacco juice, and exceedingly rude to a boy who worshiped him.

But that was in the day's work. Which he was fast learning.

He says, of those first six months, that he was most desperately lonely; that a stranger's first year in New York is apt to be about the most miserable time in his existence, and that possibly one can feel more solitary on a desert island than in the midst of five million people, none of whom you know, but he doubts it.

The people in his boardinghouse seemed to him a commonplace and depressing lot, and as he would ever prefer perishing in solitary confinement to being bored, he avoided them. He was on a morning paper, which meant that he worked nights, from two A.M. until eight or nine. He would go home and sleep and in the afternoon and in the evening take long walks, walking off his homesickness and his worry that he was not getting ahead as fast as he wanted to, and all unconsciously, by so doing, learning his city backward, forward, inside, outside, from Hell's Kitchen to Hell Gate. He worked out a plan for himself, and it's a good one for any stranger alone in a great city. He would take a streetcar, or an elevated, and ride until he came to a part of town that was unfamiliar to him, then get off and deliberately set out to lose himself. And all the while that extraordinary photographic memory of his was storing up a million impressions, the strange sights and colors and sounds and smells and types, packing them all neatly into his subconscious, ready for the day when he would take them out and use them in a hundred short stories.

Certainly I know, as surely as though I had walked by his side, that a story of his called "An Occurrence up a Side Street" (and incidentally it's a honey) came to him/ as he trudged some lonely, hot, shut street and saw the glare of Broadway lighting most luridly the blanketing sky of some stifling night. What was going on behind the dark, quiet fronts of the shuttered houses? It was fourteen years or more before he fitted a story to the sense of mystery and evil that came from them to him; the story of course was invention, but the atmosphere in which it was dipped and dyed so deeply was authentic. Oh, most chokingly, terribly authentic!

But the glory of the day when that story would appear in the *Saturday Evening Post* was a long ways away, and he not dreaming of it, but rather of Loll and me, and the chances of his ever having a home again, and after that, I guess, somebody—maybe most anybody—to talk to.

I think that about the most heartbreaking seriocomic story I know, except for the one about George Creel's coat, is Dad's account of his first Christmas in New York. Maybe George Creel's is the bitterer; at least I always broke into convulsive sobs in the places where one is supposed to laugh, because there was cruelty mixed up in his and I can never believe that cruelty is anything but deliberate.

It was like this. George had been a very poor boy. And always he had a dream that he would someday own a certain sort of coat, a coat that through the years became a magic garment to him, for it symbolized success and achievement and release from want. It was to be the most beautiful coat in the world, double-breasted, braid-bound and lined with fur, exactly like the one worn by the leading man of his home-town stock company. Ah! if he could ever own a fur-lined coat!

So by doing without lunch, and following that by a light dinner, and by stopping smoking, and walking to work, and not having any pleasures, at least not any that cost money, he saved up enough to make a down payment on his heart's desire. It was made by a cheap tailor, the cheapest he could find, and the fur was guaranteed genuine cat. But he thought it was wonderful. And it was wonderful! So he put it on and wore it to the office. And he thought he wouldn't say anything; he'd be modest and, without any braggadocio prompting from him, let the boys first get a load of his grandeur and then come around, strictly of their own accord, to envy and congratulate him and ask him where he got it, and if his rich uncle had died, or what? Well, they gathered around him, all right. And one of them did ask him how much he paid for it. "Why, good Lord, man," exclaimed this dear old kidder, "I could have got that coat for you for half the price!" And another comic said he'd be willing to take it off poor old George's hands, for as much as half what he'd paid for it, as he lived in the country and it wouldn't matter if he did look funny out there. And so on and so forth, until the boys had had their fill of the fun. So George took his coat home and never, never wore it again.

Dad's Christmas wasn't too good either. He was all alone in the boardinghouse. Everybody else there had somebody to spend the day with, even the landlady. He sat in his telephone booth of a room until late afternoon, dreaming and imagining what Laura's Christmas was like, trying to project himself way down yonder to the old house in Savannah, where I was getting my first load of my first Christmas tree and distinguishing myself by throwing up my hands in solemn awe and exclaiming, "Oh, Jesus! Sweet Jesus!" Southern babies, raised by colored nurses, can sometimes surprise their families no little.

After a while, along in a gray, cold afternoon, he could no longer bear to be alone. So he put on his coat and drifted down the street to a neighborly bar. The proprietor was a kindly old German who had talked to him sometimes when Irvin was especially lonely. He hardly expected the place to be open today, but it was, and the old man, although obviously surprised at seeing him, tried his best to make a little Christmas cheer. The drinks, today, he said, were on him. Irvin had been thinking that maybe he'd treat himself to an eggnog, or a flaming Tom and Jerry, which is what he would have been drinking if he had been home, but now he was a guest and took what he was offered, which was cold draft beer. It wasn't much fortification against the icy day and the icy hours ahead of him, and it wasn't his idea of Yuletide wassail either, but he drank it gratefully, taking a long time to do so, until a certain restiveness in his host made it known that he too had a date, and wanted to close up shop.

Then Irvin went back to his little room in the dark, silent boardinghouse, and pulling up a chair by the window just plain old wallered in loneliness and longing. And when he

was at the very lowest depths of misery he heard music. Somewhere out there in the night an optimistic organ-grinder was plying his wares . . . I mean his tune. And his tune was "My Old Kentucky Home."

After that things got better. I guess he couldn't have stood it if they hadn't. First, and foremost, he was beginning to get a little recognition, which was mighty important to him for its own sake, for it was his first and last and greatest pride that he was a good reporter. Years later he wrote, in a mood most happily and innocently vainglorious, "I am a good reporter, and I admit it and I can prove it and I am proud of it. And if you don't believe I am—why, I am, that's all!"

But he also wrote, in the same piece:
My weakest point [both as a reporter and as a fiction writer] is a tendency to over-write, to over-elaborate, a story which interests me personally. (Perhaps I am over-writing now.) My strongest point is a sense of news values. . . . My heaviest liability in the line of outstanding repertorial shortcomings is an almost complete absence of the deductive quality, wherefore effects appeal to me rather than causes. As an analyst I would never shine unless it were with the same shininess which we associate with a brass dime.

I think he was perfectly right about this. Certainly in his stories, although he dealt so often with the macabre and the sinister, it was always as a reporter—that is, one who tells the facts and only the facts, and from them deduces the characters which have created these facts, instead of the other way round. And when he stopped seeing things, just like Kipling, one of the greatest reporters, he stopped creating. From then on he could only remember. I don't know why he stopped seeing. I only know that he did. Somewhere along the road he grew tired. The film ran out, the camera was only a little empty black box. It was a tragedy to him.

It was a long winter, but it passed at last and then he and Laura began tentatively planning on the day when she could join him. There was much writing back and forth, much adding up of sums of money, and of weeks, and then days, and finally hours.

They figured that if all three of us lived in one room in the boardinghouse that they could manage, and then they discovered that somewhere along the line they had most frightfully undercalculated and were still three dollars a week shy. Despair from Irvin: but Laura wrote not to be silly, that she would do not three, but four dollars a week's worth of laundry, and was catching the next train north.

In those prehistoric days there was no Pennsylvania Station. One was put off the train in Jersey and then took a ferryboat. Irvin was so excited that he got to the terminus hours before the train could possibly arrive, and then finding himself with nothing to do bought a magazine with which to while away the time that seemed as though it would never, never pass. Composing himself with an effort of the will, he settled down to read. Now when he read, then or later, he instantly became entirely unconscious of everything else. Small boys could march over his lap beating on large drums, Indian braves could disembowel a record catch of victims directly in front of him, and when he came out of his book he'd have to be told about the doings, yes, and be sore and sorry that he hadn't seen and heard them too!

So Laura's train was announced. He read on. It arrived. He still read on. She waited and waited, shifting a large, weary, unhappy baby from arm to arm. He read. She gathered up the bags and the big box of goodies for him and the baby's affairs, and very scared and very mad, captured a porter and got herself on the ferry and over to New York and into a cab and up to the boardinghouse and into the room and me in bed and fed and was beginning on her unpacking. And he came to the end of his story.

She says that she heard first the *cloppity-clop* of the cab, then the sound of its stopping in front of the house, and knew that he had come at last. She was holding a large jar of pickled shrimps in her hand, which she had brought him as a treat, and she was in half a mind to drop this on his head as a reminder that he not only had a wife, but one on hand and boiling mad to boot. But he just fairly fell out of that cab, and as he was so doing at the same instant he was reaching for his money, and he always carried this all bunched up in his hip pocket, so as he fell, it fell and he had to scurry around and rescue it, all the time looking most wild and desperate. This performance was so characteristic and so touching that she decided not to drop the pickled shrimps on him after all. Still, and even so, there was going to be a coolness to his welcome, not so much coolness as she had originally planned (indeed this would have frozen him so stiff that he could be broken up and used for ice cubes) but still some.

She heard him running up the stairs, stumbling in his haste, and then he jerked open the door, and stood there with his miserable guilty face all puckered up. And so she ran to him and put her arms around him and burst into tears. I guess it was a pretty good reunion after all.

But she always discouraged him from meeting her after that.

That evening they took a walk to see the town, and from that hour there was never going to be any doubt in her mind that she had found her place. My, my, how little Southern girls do love New York! She squeezed his arm ecstatically.

"Think you're going to like it, Loll?"

"I'm crazy about it."

"How can you be so sure?"

"Why, because now I can get to know all the common people I want to," she explained.

As this was about the last ambition he had ever suspected her of cherishing, he was astounded, and said so.

"Well, down home," Laura explained, "you know we were never allowed to know anybody unless everybody had known their grandmothers and grandfathers. I always thought it was so stupid. From now on I'm never going to ask who anybody's grandfather was, and if anybody asks me I'm going to say I didn't have one."

Coming home, arm in arm, she suddenly said something else that astonished him.

"There's something else I've learned tonight," she stated.

"And what's that?"

"I've learned what a 'hard face' is."

"What?"

"All my life I've heard people talking about somebody or other having a 'hard face.' And I never knew what they were talking about. I've been looking around tonight. And now I know what a 'hard face' is. I don't think I want one."

"Maybe that's a New York face. And maybe you won't be so crazy about this town as you think."

"Oh, yes, I will," said Laura. And she was. But she never got a hard face.

Of course at first she was pretty near as lonely as he had been. He was still working nights, which meant that he had to sleep most of the day. She would take me into the park, so that he might rest without disturbance, and pushing the baby carriage, would look, wistfully enough, at the crowds of people and wonder how one ever got to know anybody, common or not, in this great, indifferent, rushing, preoccupied place. Then she'd go home for lunch at the boardinghouse and if Irvin happened to wake they would eat together. In the afternoons she went back to the park. They had dinner and then he read awhile, or maybe took a nap, and then went to work. It wasn't what you'd call a gay, mad life exactly. It paid off, though. He thought she was wonderful. For the rest of his days every time he got good and mad at her, he'd go take a long walk, and when he came home he'd have been remembering those days and how blithe and sweet she had been through them, and then he would permit himself to be forgiven for being in the right, and her to do anything that had come into her head.

"All right . . . all right. Damn it all, Lolly . . . all right!" and quoting Oliver Herford: "It's just a whim . . . but my wife has a whim of iron."

For her part she always thought that he was pretty much entitled to do anything he liked, too. She thought he had earned it. . . . All in all, they had a fine feeling between them, and as time goes by and the big young adventure is behind one, I guess that's an awful lot. Here I mean the word "awful" in its strictest sense. I mean awe-inspiring, and wonderful. A tough time shared by two people in love can make a tough bond, so tough and strong that it is not to be broken easily, if at all. Older folks usually know this, and so it's a strange thing that they are so often scared limber at the thought of their children going through the things that they went through, right in their stride. At least mine were. And I am.

It was during those weeks that there arose the great problem of who was going to discipline Buff (that's me, so called because a nurse, rebelling at the length of the name Elisabeth had announced: "Lisabuff!—Dat one great big ole pompious name for a little ole scrap of a baby. I jus' calls her Buff.") The question of who was to do the disciplining was never solved, because Dad always insisted that my mother transform herself into a stern, firm parent, and then landed on her, like a pan of milk from the top shelf, whenever she tried it.

This time they led me into the dining room one noon, and when I was informed that for lunch there was lamb chop, baked potato and ice cream, I announced blandly that just a little ice cream would do for me. They could give the lamb chop and the baked potato to someone who cared for such things. I would make *my* meal with " 'ert" (dessert).

"No, Buff," said Laura. "Baked pota-to, and lamb chop first . . . then 'ert." I didn't waste any time arguing with that woman; I just opened my mouth and hollered—even at that tender age having all the necessary equipment for really sensational sound effects. I was led howling upstairs, convoyed by both exasperated parents, the male one insisting that on *no* conditions was I to be allowed to get away with it. So Laura spanked me. Then she asked me if I'd eat my baked potato and my lamb chop before my 'ert, and I said, gulping hard but still in there pitching, that I would not. So then she spanked me. And then she asked me again. And then she spanked me . . . And then she asked me . . . Dad went for a walk around the block. She thinks she spanked me five times, and by then she was as unhappy and distracted, if not quite as sore, as I. At last I gave in and was returned to society and the ministrations of my pal, Bessie the waitress. "Bessie," said I, seating myself, "I'll just have a little 'ert for my lunch."

Laura, weeping, rose from her place, ready to start all over again, upon which I summoned up a very watery smile, very quickly, and stammered, "Oh, Bessie . . . some people around here can't take a joke!"

Fine! Laura had won that round, as per instructions received. Later she reported as much to the returned Irvin, expecting, maybe, a little comforting herself, because while I had gone smack off to sleep, after having eaten *all* my lunch, her insides were still quivering like a hummingbird in a hurry.

Did she get it? Not so as you could notice it! He told her she was a brutal woman. He—he blasted her with wrath!

"All right," said she. "Next time she needs spanking . . . *you* do it."

"I will not," said he. "Certainly not! That's your job."

They weren't getting anywhere fast. And never did.

Spring wore on into an early hot summer. I grew querulous and pale, and Laura found herself shuddering with loathing for that dusty, stifling park. They had begun to pile work on Irvin all of a sudden, and the lady in the room next door took to practicing on the piano of a morning, so that he couldn't sleep. Laura began to dream nights, and days too, of Tybee Beach—blue water and silver sand, and her mama's clean, sweet-smelling, cool cottage, and old Fanny Whitaker's deviled crabs and icebox rolls, and the lane of oleanders that she had planted down the boardwalk, and of the baby growing brown and merry from paddling in the salt shallows.

And Irvin began to dream of ways and means to murder a piano player without being hanged for it.

At last one night he came home with news of a boarding-house at a seaside resort. A man at the office had told him about it, saying that it was cheap and comfortable. They left the very next afternoon, and arrived in the early evening. They found the place without any trouble, which was a good thing, laden down as they were with babe and belongings.

"Here we are at last!" said Irvin, pushing the bell.

"I don't like it," said Laura.

"For the love of heaven, Lolly!" said Irvin. "How do you know you don't like it? You aren't even inside the place yet. Are you packing a Ouija board on your person? Or harking to the voice of Little Princess Running-Nose, your spirit guide?"

"It's not clean," said Laura.

"How can you possibly know that it is not clean?"

"I can smell flies," she said. "And stale grease."

"Through a closed door?"

"Through two closed doors. Through ten closed doors. Through anything."

"That's right," said Irvin. "Start kicking before you even get inside."

He settled us and then, as he had to go back to town and work, left. The next morning, confirmed in her darkest fears regarding those flies and that grease, she got me ready for the beach. At least the sea would be cool and clean. All the rest of the boarders were gathered on the front porch as she went out, the men in their undershirts, the women in curlpapers. Early as it was, there was already a motion afoot to "rush the growler." One of the ladies, prodded into action by her spouse, was starting off, still attached to her curlpapers, which may have been indigenous, and armed with a large tin pail.

Shuddering to her Savannah, Georgia, boot heels, Laura made her way down to the beach where she spent the rest of the day, not even returning for lunch or my nap. She began to think she had been a little rash when she announced that from now on it would be her delight to know all "common" people; certainly she felt no passionate desire to go back to that boardinghouse and mingle with those that were all too available at the moment.

Irvin did not get out that night. She put me to bed and sat in the dark with every nerve quivering like her poor little, fastidious, distended nostrils, and then she too went to bed and asleep. She was awakened by lights being suddenly snapped on to see Irvin with the most radiant and transfigured face, leaning over the foot of her bed and beaming at her.

"Oh, what is it? What is it, darling?" she cried.

"It's the big break, Lolly! My chance. The paper is sending

me to the Peace Conference at Portsmouth, as a special correspondent, with a by-line and all." Then his face clouded over.
"But I didn't think, Lolly! I can't take it! I can't leave you in
this dump."

"Can you raise the price for a ticket to Savannah?" she demanded.

"I can borrow it."

"Then Buff and I will go tomorrow.... No. Wait! ... We'll
go today! Starting now!"

"You don't mind going back?"

"Darling," said Laura, pulling a suitcase down from a shelf.
"It will only be for the time you're at the conference and ...
no, I don't mind going back. It'll just be going back to heaven
—that's all!"

"And," says she, "when I walked down the path between
the oleanders, and Fanny Whitaker came running out to take
you over, I knew I'd been right. It *was* heaven!"

It was pretty paradisial for Irvin too, up there in the nice old
New England town, where T. R. the Great had maneuvered
the Russians and the Japs into holding a conference. For the
first time since he had come north he was making some friends,
chief among them the famous Charley Hand of the London
Daily Mail, and Sam Blythe, who once was a Washington
pundit and is now Sage and Saviour of the California red-
woods, and was a club mate and pal for all the years from then
until last March. More important, or so it seemed then, he was
making a genuine hit on the paper with the stories he was sending back.

Bob Davis, who knew him then, or very shortly after then,
wrote this about his work:

Cobb cast his experienced eye over the situation, discovered
that the story was already well covered by a large coterie of

competent, serious-minded young men, and went into action to write a few columns daily on subjects having no bearing whatsoever on the conference. . . . There wasn't a single fact in the entire series, and yet The Sun syndicated them throughout the United States.

So he had been right. It was the big break, the big chance. As they say in the mountains, he was going "Wake Snakes! And Ginral Jackson Fit the Indians!" And he knew it, and the paper knew it, and what was greatly to the point, the paper did something about it too, so that the boardinghouse on West Fifty-seventh knew them no more. They became house, or at least apartment-holders up on West One Hundred and Forty-sixth street, living grandly "in their own furniture," as the French say. Pretty soon they grew very splendid and had a part-time maid to take me out in the afternoons and get dinner and whatnot. In the same building they found friends, Helen and Harry Burke. Harry was a newspaperman too, and Helen the most exquisite and enchanting little person. Then pretty young Manie, the kid sister, came up from Paducah, and all the lonely days were over.

Of course it wasn't *all* beer and skittles. For instance, there were those part-time maids, then as now, uppity, independent and very part-time indeed! Here today—and gone today! They received in those incredible days four dollars a week for their very own. And did the laundry. And my hat is certainly off to anyone who can stay uppity on four dollars a week—and do the laundry!

One of those who became, briefly, an old Cobb family retainer was an engaging damsel, very black, and when she reported for her first day's work, very drunk too. It was Monday, washday. After doing the laundry she tugged it up to the roof, but lingered there only long enough to pin up one poor

wet sheet before descending precipitately, leaving the wash
behind her to look after itself, and announcing that she was
quitting, and right now too. When pressed, with some anguish, for a reason, she proclaimed her discovery that "De
wind do blow from de ribber on de roof" . . . and she'd take
her week's pay and go now. Please, ma'am.

"You mean your day's pay?"

"No, ma'am, I does not. I means my week's pay."

Well, she didn't get it, but it took an elevator boy, and the
threat of calling a cop, to remove her from the premises without it. She was last seen weaving up the street and giving her
opinion of her late employers in a voice clearly audible for
several city blocks.

Harry Burke, coming home from work, encountered her,
and dropped by to tell Laura about the funny darky he'd just
seen, and heard. Oh, very distinctly heard!

"She was screaming her head off," he said, chuckling, "and
shouting, 'Dey got de cut glass, and dey got de silver—but dey
de poor white trash all de same!' Wonder who she'd been
working for? Must be mighty funny people!"

"Wonder no more," said Laura. "The mighty funny people
are us."

And then the Thaw trial broke. Of this Dad says:

Editors and reporters are forever dreaming of the perfect
murder story, which will be the story of a young and pretty
woman, preferably an actress, accused of killing a rich man by
poisoning him, with a lot of mystifying features and compli-
cations to go along with it. When this comes to pass, if it ever
does, it will be, from the standpoint of public interest (which
means circulation . . .) a faultless story.

Of course he wrote this before the Lindbergh baby was
murdered by Bruno Hauptmann, and I guess (and mind you,

I too am speaking not from the humanitarian point of view, but strictly from circulation) that if that greedy, murderous Heinie, Hauptmann, had not been an out-of-work carpenter but a famous, or even notorious person, the story from the editors' angle would have been "improved." (And God forgive me for using the word!)

But the Thaw case certainly had a lot. A young millionaire kills a famous genius upon the top of New York's most noted building, a building which was itself a creation of the victim, during the opening performance of a summer roof-garden show, with an audience of Broadway first-nighters for eye-witnesses. One certainly must admit that wasn't bad.

Irvin was one of the reporters at the trial. And here he hung up what he always believed was some sort of a record, for he wrote in longhand a running story of the trial as it proceeded minute by minute, catching what was happening as it happened, at the same time that he was putting down a synthesis of that which had gone before, and this included the high spots of the testimony, answers, questions, objections, byplays and high lights, besides all the local color that he could crowd in. He wrote over five hundred thousand words before it was over, or roughly the equivalent of eight summer novels. And suffered so from the strain that a saber-toothed tiger with an abscessed molar might equal, but would not excel, the ferocity of his disposition.

It was getting on toward the end of the trial, and of his strength, when Laura smote him with a fried egg. Soft-fried— sunny side up. Which took his mind off Harry Thaw right away, and was a good thing all round.

It happened like this. She was trying to get his breakfast and feed me and help him dress, all at the same time, and every time she'd get started on one thing he'd yell for her to drop it and take up another.

He started it by demanding to know whether he had any clean shirts, and if not, why not, and if so, why were they concealed from him, and if concealed, where?

"Your clean shirts, Irvin," she called, "are right where they always are. Of course."

He appeared, blood in his eye. "Nothing in this house is ever where it always is. I demand that you come and find my clean shirts. At once."

"If I do," she said, "the eggs will burn."

With a growl of pure hate he retreated, to return again almost instantly with some further beef. Indeed he produced one for each and every item of his wardrobe.

At last, dressed, and to some extent in his right mind, he was ready to eat. And just as Laura was about to give him his food the dumb-waiter bell rang. She went to answer it, carrying his eggs, in a distracted manner, with her.

"Are you, or are you not, going to give me those eggs?" he demanded.

"I am," said she. And did so. Smack in the puss!

She repented at once, and helped him to dress all over again, weeping from repentance the while. . . . Indeed she continued to weep, at intervals, all day. And Manie said she was sorry to have to say it but that honestly she did think it was the most awful, the commonest thing that she had ever seen a person do, that in her wildest dreams she had never expected to know a woman who would hit a poor, tired, overworked husband with a fried egg. And Laura agreed.

But next morning he started in on Manie (being slightly wary of Laura, I guess) and *she* hit him with a big, juicy grapefruit!

"The next time I try to eat breakfast in this house," he said, "I'm going to wear a catcher's mask."

And as soon as the trial was over it was decided that it might be a good idea for Irvin to take a little trip. Alone.

He went to Cuba, and when he returned, very sheepish, and *very* glad to see the girls, he found that because of his work he had become a local celebrity in a minor way, and things, both professionally and socially, began to open up for him. For instance, he and Laura and Manie were invited to one of Robert Chanler's famous parties. (Yes—that same Robert Chanler who was later on to marry Lina Cavalieri and from his brother in the booby hatch receive the famous telegram reading: "WHOSE LOONY NOW?")

Up on One Hundred and Forty-sixth Street was an enormous to-do about getting ready for the party. Neither of the girls had evening clothes, so they had to be made for the occasion. They were little white frocks run up by a "little" dressmaker—and looking it—then slippers had to be provided, and gloves, after careful, careful bargain-hunting, which even so most savagely shattered the budget. Of course, evening coats were out of the question.

They took the subway from the apartment to Greenwich Village where Chanler lived and then, grandly, hired a cab to drive from the sub station to his door. Both the girls, I guess—certainly Laura—were feeling very shy and small-town and scared as they stood on the steps waiting to be let in, and Irvin cheered them no little by first looking them over carefully and then remarking that the way they looked made him feel like he was delivering the week's wash!

Laura says that she will never forget that evening. She retreated at once to a window seat which was mercifully draped with curtains sufficiently voluminous for her to hide behind, but she did peek out. Everybody looked wonderful to her, but May Wilson Preston looked so very wonderful that she was dazzled beyond envy, and awed beyond coherent cerebration. She told me, only yesterday, what May wore—down to the buckles on her shoes. They were diamond. Besides these she had a white Irish-lace dress, princess-style, with a high neck and enormous sleeves, and a bird of paradise in her hair. She was just back from Paris. Since May was then, as she is now, divine-looking, she almost paralyzed Laura. In the years to come May and Laura would go shopping together in Paris, but I don't suppose that all the *couturières* there ever were, put together, could design anything so gorgeous as Laura thought that white lace dress. Maybe when she gets to heaven she will find one as beautiful, but short of the pearly gates she might as well stop looking.

Next day I guess Dad repented of his remark about the week's wash. Anyhow he laid some deep plans, and all secretive and full of low cunning, began holding out lunch money and cigar money on himself until he had a sufficient sum laid by, and then he up and spent it all on a dress for Laura.

Wow! That *was* a dress! It was "princess-style," of course, and made of very heavy white silk, with great zigzag stripes of bright green, starting at the neck and broadening as they descended to a wide and evil end at the hem line. Funny sort of stripes, looking rather as though they had been cut out of an overripe watermelon rind and then pasted on.

It was a dress for a six-footer with a bold bosom . . . or maybe a female impersonator. Poor little Laura! Five-two in her high heels and, as Joe Mullen swears he heard his mother say of an aunt, "A nice girl . . . but she never fills her blouse."

I remember that dress very tenderly because much later on it became the queen's robe when theatricals were given in our attic. I thought it was very beautiful, just as beautiful as Dad did.

When he brought it home, Laura took one look and broke into tears.

He was crushed. "You don't like it!"

"Of course I like it!"

"Why are you crying then?"

"Because I never hoped to own anything so lovely, of course. It's the p-p-p-prettiest dress I ever saw!"

Gallant little liar! And she did not stop at lying. She wore it. For many, many years.

It was about then that Irvin made a remark which was quoted a lot, and still is, although attributed to almost everybody from Petronius to Parker. He was told one morning by the elevator boy in the office that his boss Charlie Chapin, whom he and everybody else detested, was ill, and Irvin said, "Indeed? Well, let's hope it's nothing trivial!"

There's a funny thing about a funny line. It can die a-borning, or it can live so long and so persistently that its creator gets so sick of it he feels like taking a stick and beating its head in; it can be spoken under some circumstances and rate nary a laugh, but, if repeated under different auspices, rock the company and win that queer but fascinating kind of fame which gives one passport to the company of those "in the know"—the bright girls and boys, who knowing all the old ones, by the same token can sense the arrival of a new star long before its light is visible to the multitude. It's a heady kind of fame, and can peter out mighty quick, and be most destructive in its petering. Just let an artist start playing to the gang, and grow scornful of the uninitiate, and two will get you ten—he's a blowed-up sucker!

Irvin himself wrote:

A really funny idea has a long, long life and a merry one. I've known funny ideas that had grown sixteen rattles and a button, and were still wagging along steadily.... A humorist working by the day at Denver, Colorado, we will say, has a funny idea. It's a bully funny idea. It comes to him like a bolt from the blue . . . all of a sudden—bang! there is the idea sloshing around in his brain, making trouble for all the old settler ideas that have been there all along. It is a noble and a precious and a priceless thing, and he figures he ought to get as much as seventy-five cents for it.

Then he goes on to trace what will happen to that lovely notion. An editor and a printer and a proofreader all have a little fling at it, but finally it sees the light of day, and takes its foot in its hand and starts on its travels.

A paragrapher packs it down into a line. A versifier stretches it into a jingle. A columnist turns it into a bit of repartee. By turns it is an anecdote, a bon mot, an after-dinner speech, a popular song, an apt retort, a catch line, a space filler, a set of verses, a slogan and a parody.

Then it gets grand. It becomes a musical comedy, a movie— a whole lot of movies.

But the end is not yet. In the meanwhile it has crossed the seas to the Mother Country, where, after being carefully sterilized, deodorized, searched for concealed deadly points, disinfected, and furnished with footnotes, a chart, a glossary, and a set of plans and specifications, it becomes a regular English joke and appears in *Punch*. It is then copied back on this side by the *Evening Post*. . . . And then some hoary-headed old doodlebug of an antiquarian crawls out from under a log in the woods and produces the proof to show that it was stolen from Charles Lamb, who got it from Aristophanes, who copied it from one of the Pyramids, but after that its real origin is lost in the mists of prehistoric times.

For when all is said and done, real humor is even as bread cast upon the waters—it returns to you after many days with somebody else's name signed to it.

He ought to know, for it was about now that he was upped, or downed, depending how you look at it, into being a columnist on the New York *World*.

At the same time he began to plump up. One day he was a long, lean, Gary-Cooper-legged boy, the next a fat man.

In his column, "New York Through Funny Glasses," he gave this description of himself:

To be perfectly frank with you, Cobb is related to my wife by marriage. I should say that in appearance he is rather bulky, standing six feet high, not especially beautiful, a light roan in color, with a black mane. His figure is undecided, but might be called bunchy in spots. He has always, like his father who was a Confederate soldier, voted the Democratic ticket. He has had one wife and one child and still has them. In religion he is an innocent bystander.

He meant this, about being an innocent bystander, and kept on meaning it. And sure did get jumped on for saying so! I've seen the clippings, among the few that he kept, of interviews with prominent clergymen, and every last one of them coming down on him like a lion on a duck. He did not mean to offend anyone. It was only that he had revolted from the strict—and by his standards—cruel theology of his youth and found no other creed, in the churchly sense, to satisfy him.

I remember his saying to me, one day just before we left Santa Monica, that he wasn't worried—much—about the hereafter. He guessed that if one's personality continued on into some other world, when one arrived there one would be like a child, and there would be somebody to show you the ropes, while if this was all the life that was to be given one, well, that was all right by him. He needed a good long rest anyhow.

He ran "Funny Glasses" for four or five years, supplying the evening edition and the Sunday magazine with a comic feature.

Then he wrote the book for a musical comedy, done to order in five days. He says that only the absence of a guillotine in New York State accounts for his escape for the offense. I have read it. He is quite right. It was indeed a narrow escape. And down south they would have lynched him.

But we were getting in the chips now, so we bought a house in a suburb. I guess, maybe, it was my odd behavior that accelerated the move, because I began coming home from the park with long, and evidently very convincing, stories of some new playmates who were called Silo, Philo and Spinach. Spinach was a little girl with long golden curls. My mother began to think that I was getting to know some very odd people indeed. It wasn't until afterward that she discovered Silo, Philo and Spinach were going to move with us, they being entirely figments of my imagination. And terribly, terribly, tiresome ones at that! But it was too late then. We had already, in our usual mad search for the true Bohemia, moved to Yonkers.

Chapter 3

WHAT ARE YONKERS?

YONKERS are a state of mind. Also a manufacturing city not far from New York. Later on Dad said that he moved there because it reminded him of the two towns that he knew and loved best, it having all the metropolitan gaiety of Paducah, Kentucky, and all the truly rural charm of New York. (Any posse of enraged citizens from Yonkers will kindly remember, before stringing *me* up, that it was my Pa who said that.)

And we weren't really even true Yonkers (or Yonketts, or Yonks, or whatever is the correct designation for them as hails from that no-doubt justly outraged community), for we lived in Park Hill, which is a suburb and a very pretty one.

We were making the regular trek, of course. That's the way it goes for young marrieds. They come to New York. They live in a little makeshift apartment, way uptown or way downtown, they set up a baby, then move to a suburb, then back to town—only now the address is fancier, then back to the country—only this time it is the real country, really expensive and really inconvenient and really something.

Later on my folks grew very sniffy about privacy and views and amusing neighbors, and stuff, but this time they were only sniffy about the price. And when they found a house they could buy cheap, they bought it. It wasn't a pretty house but it had lovely plumbing. Indeed it had been built and outfitted by a plumber for his own delectation.

It was a plain little box of a house, with a porch stuck on front, awkward as a prop mustache at a fancy-dress party, but under Laura's handling it was pretty and comfortable inside, while outside our plot possessed three fine natural features. To the left of the house was an outcropping of rock, bigger than a mere boulder, for if one were very small one had to scramble and climb a bit to gain the heights, and it was thus precisely the right size and shape to serve as a ship, a fortress or a house; an apartment house really, for half the kids in the neighborhood staked out a claim to certain declivities and smooth hollows along its sides and on top. A hospitable rock, easy to colonize and to defend. On the right of our house, "Second Mortgage Hall," was a sunny little strip of ground, free of pesky tree roots, where the first of Laura's gardens was laid out, and in the back yard was one magnificent pine tree, a lonely old patriarch of a tree, left solitary there when a noble grove was cleared away sometime or other.

Our lot was fifty feet wide and a hundred deep. That's a fine demesne, at once ample, convenient and varied, when it contains a rock, a garden and a tree.

I don't think that they had a very good time in Park Hill. This was probably more their fault than Park Hill's for they had had a taste of the company of those who were doing the same kind of work, in this case creative work. And everybody loves to talk "shop"—if it's one's own shop—and after having once enjoyed it are going to be happier, or at least easier, with those who can speak their language without the aid of an interpreter.

But me, I had a fine time. First place I discovered God. I had never been sent to Sunday school, because my family had had too much Sunday school in their day and so were in revolt against organized religion, but out in Park Hill, finding that all the kids went somewhere on Sunday mornings and not wanting to miss anything, I solemnly dressed myself up and tagged along with the bunch to see what gave. I didn't miss a trick—I mean a church. From the synagogue to the Catholic chapel they made me welcome, odd little visitant that I was, which I think very swell of them indeed. I don't remember much of this pilgrimage, for of course that's what it was, but I do remember being invited, or more likely inviting myself, to a Sunday-afternoon gathering at the house of that wonderful woman, Belle Israels Moskowitz, who later on was to get into all sorts of benevolent hanky-panky with Al Smith. She read the Bible, and then explained what she had read, simply and most eloquently, to her own children and to a fascinated small stranger, and I carried home the news that something pretty terrific was going on down the street on Sunday afternoons, so when the next one came around Laura and Irvin went with me, and forever after thanked me for the experience, and for a friend.

It was I who first brought them the Dorans too. The Doran family had moved into the house directly in back of us and I had been one of the small fry who gathered to help settle them in. Moving vans are almost as interesting as new houses, of course, and there are all kinds of loot, like sawdust and string and broken bits and pieces to be garnered from both, though you don't find those beautiful blonde curls of shavings, a most valuable treasure, in moving vans. I remember we were deeply impressed with the Dorans. I told the family they were lovely people, and when asked why I thought so said it was because they had such swell garbage.

It turned out they had more than that. They had a publishing firm. It was George H. Doran then, Doubleday, Doran now, and when Dad had a first book published it was the Doran Company that did the deed.

I begin to remember my father now—I was six—and like

most people, I think, have no recollection dating before then that has not strictly to do with myself. But he becomes a person to me on one afternoon, in autumn—yes, pretty sure to have been autumn—for there is the scent of burning leaves in the air, and I am calling out to some children, "My Dad is home . . . my Dad is home!" And I am running very fast and thinking, "How fast I can run! . . . I am wonderful to be able to run so fast!"

And Dad swings me off the ground and says, and I suppose this is why the memory is so vivid, "My! . . . What a big girl! . . . You were running like a deer!" To fix a moment in a woman's head there is nothing like nailing it there with a compliment!

I wish that I could remember the Sunday afternoons back in Paducah, when he amused and touched the whole town by packing me onto a pillow and toting me all over town to pay calls and be admired. Everybody laughed and said Irvin was plain imbecile about that baby, and loved him for being so.

The next memory that I have of him must have been later because it is not quite so egotistical. It was a hot summer afternoon, and probably he was taking his vacation, for else how was it that I was lying by his side in a darkened room in the daytime? He was never home in the daytime, except on Sundays, and this has no Sunday "feel." No—it was an unusual occasion and I remember it as such. He read me the first story from *The Jungle Book*. He read wonderfully, leaving me gasping with the thrill of that trip to the Seeonee Wolf-pack's cave in the hills. Lordy! Lordy! This minute I can hear Shere Khan roaring from the pain of his burned foot, and for his lost prey, Mowgli the Frog. Yes, and long for that broad kind back to cuddle against, and take comfort from, as I suffer a most luscious sort of fear!

When he stopped reading I assaulted him. It was intolerable

that all, *all,* that book be not read to me now, at once, straight through and without stopping! He swung me in the air, laughing, while I spit with fury. "I know, kid . . . I know!" he said.

That is a fine memory.

Later on when he used to read to me, from books of my choosing, such as the *Rover Boys,* he developed a most annoying trick of interpolating, annoying to me, that is, for they do say that he would send any more adult listeners into shrieks of mirth, but my shrieks were louder than anyone's . . . and they weren't of mirth either! Ah me! "Fun-loving Sam" did take an awful beating from I. S. C. . . . And I was *so* in love with Sam! I still think it was a dirty trick, and as for what he did to *Ramona!* Well, it shouldn't happen to a dog!

It was a particularly brutal business because, by this time, I could read myself and his attention was drawn to the long-suffering Indian maid only because I turned up for my supper with a face so swollen from weeping that I looked as though I were coming down with something more than usually malignant. Ramona had a hell of a time with Alessandro, her Indian lover, but her sufferings with him were as nothing compared to what she went through when Irvin began remolding her destiny.

I have found a fine portrait of him at this time, from the hand of his beloved pal, Bob Davis. Bob wrote:

The first glimpse I had of him was in a half-tone picture in the New York *Evening World*. This portrait hung pendant-like from a title which read "New York through Funny Glasses" by Irvin S. Cobb. It was the face of a man scarred with uncertainty; an even money proposition that he had just emerged from the Commune or was about to enter it. Grief was written on the brow; more than written—it was emblazoned. The eyes were heavy with inexpressible sadness. The corners of the mouth drooped, heightening the whole effect of incomprehensible sadness. Quickly I turned to the next page among the stock quotations, where I got my depression in a blanket form. The concentrated Cobb was too much for me.

A few days later I suddenly came upon the face again. The very incongruity of its alliance with laughter overwhelmed me, and wonderingly I read what he had written, always with the handicap of that half-tone. If Cobb were an older man I would go on the witness stand and swear that the photograph was made when he was witnessing the Custer Massacre or the passing of Geronimo through the winter quarters of his enemies. Notwithstanding he supplied my week's laughter from then on.

I guess he kept the laughter for the column those days. Arnold Bennett once wrote that he always added to the prayer "for those in peril on the sea" a plea "for those finishing first novels." Irvin would most certainly nominate for the company which stands in need of prayer those writing a daily column, especially a would-be humorous one.

I remember a nosy neighbor asking me if my father wasn't Cobb the humorist, and when I said that I was not quite sure what a humorist was, she explained that he was one who made people laugh, an entertaining person. I shook my head positively.

"That can't be my Daddy," I said. "He's never bery entertaining round the house with me and my Moie." That is what I called Laura because she had announced that her baby was to call her "Mother" with no abbreviations, and Dad said, "Nonsense! You're too little to be called Mother—I'm going to teach her to call you 'Ma!'" And he did, but it came out Moie, and so much her name from then on that there must be many people who have never known that she was christened Laura.

Poor Dad! When he was cross it was because he was tired,

and now he was overworking again, almost as badly as during the Thaw trial days. . . .

That was the reason that one winter my mother and I were shipped off to Savannah. Everybody needed a little rest from everybody.

It was a terrific business, getting the house closed and us and Dad packed up, and attending to all the thousand and one things that turn up to plague suburban householders. To help her Laura had one Segunda, an exceptionally small and exceptionally stupid Filipino schoolboy, aged about sixteen and weighing about sixty pounds, soaking wet. So Irvin announced that he would stay home from the office and help her. She tried to dissuade him, but that only hurt his feelings, so he was on hand, ready to be helpful on the day of the hegira.

Now with his hands he was the most useless man who ever lived. From that day dates my knowledge that Irvin Cobb would help you to the very best of his considerable abilities if he was fond of you and thought you needed it, or indeed not particularly fond of you but having you brought to his attention. He'd engineer a jail break, pay off your mortgage, mind your kids, correct your manuscript, do your homework, finance your imbecile invention for turning sea water into gold, or gold into sea water, which was more usually the case with us, bury your dead and adopt your orphans, but it was better, much better, to confine his benevolent activities to such fields and refrain from asking him to open a can of beans. First place he couldn't; second place, if he tried anyhow, natural exasperation at his own ineptitude enraged him; third place, if forced to employ any tool of any description, there was going to be an accident. He could get a nutpick out of order. Arm him with tools, gadgets, can openers, ropes, shovels, any mechanical devices or dull blunt instruments, and before he was done he would not only have managed to scar himself all up—but also all and sundry who dared approach within twenty feet of him.

Why, I remember well the wail of anguish he emitted once when attempting to turn off the victrola. He had stabbed himself severely in the arm with the needle, and when I went to his rescue he quite inadvertently got me with it. And got me good! I never have figured out just how he managed that one.

And the picture lingers of his being rowed around and around a lake by Geraldine Farrar, justly indignant at being put to such labor, but, as she said, indignant or not, quite unable to bear the sight of him trying to row the boat himself.

Down in Mexico on a hunting trip we all took turns getting out of the car and opening the ten trillion gates that beset the path of travelers through the ranch country. It's a damned nuisance, so to keep peace and joy among the company all shared in the task—all except Irvin. After two or three attempts at opening and closing the simplest of gates he was so bruised and torn and sore, in more ways than one, that we got soft and let him off.

Strangely enough he could build a quick, neat fire and was beyond all limits vain of the ability.

So you see just how much use he was to Laura and the unhappy Segunda that busy blizzardy morning in February; and they with ten thousand things to do, and Irvin getting in the way of every single one of them.

Finally he had a really helpful idea. He would, he announced, descend from the bedroom window, creep down the sloping porch roof and cut the ice out of the gutters with a small ax. They were new copper gutters, very expensive, and the ice was ruining them. Laura suggested that if he left the ice where it was eventually the sun would take care of it, but he insisted that it must be done now and by him. Then she asked him if he were going to spend the rest of the winter suspended thus on the roof, because it was more than likely that unless he went on twenty-four-hour duty there the ice would form again.

He said women did not understand about such things, and stopping Segunda from continuing with whatever useful task he had been put to, sent him down to the cellar to find a good stout rope. This took quite a time, but at last one was unearthed. It had been earmarked for a packing box—but no matter! Then Irvin tied one end of the rope around his waist and giving the other end to Segunda to hold, inched himself down the slippery, steep roof to the gutter, the idea being that if he lost his footing and started to fall Segunda, and the rope, would save him. At this date he must have weighed close on two hundred and forty pounds. Segunda had but small faith in his abilities to arrest catastrophe if it threatened, but he was a good, game kid. He held on tight to his end of the rope and yelled loudly. Laura leaned out to ask them how soon should she send down a St. Bernard dog with a flask of brandy, and he told her to stop being such a fool, as he was in no mood for bum jokes right then.

Well, they do say that though he did not manage to disturb any ice he cut that new copper guttering into very small, neat pieces. The man who repaired it told everybody he'd never seen a finer job. Why, it was just in ribbons! And a bad day for the work, mind you, and only a very small ax employed throughout the entire operation!

And now there came the second big break in his career, the first, of course, being the move from the small town to the big one, the second, and equally significant one, being his quitting newspaper work for an attempt to earn his living as a writer of fiction.

Again he was prodded by Laura and sustained by her faith. I think that he never realized how important this was to him because he knew that she was not at all "literary," and therefore not a competent judge of his creative abilities. In other words he felt that though she had infinite faith in him as a man, editors of magazines might still fail to find his work up to standard. He was a good husband, and a good father; it did not follow that he was a good short-story writer.

This is a very interesting point to me; is the blind faith, the ignorant faith, of one's partner of any value? I think that it is—infinitely valuable, both as a prod and as a basic spiritual reservoir of strength. After all, critics, those pigeons on the monument, we have with us always. They will be amply provided, both those self-elected, and others specifically hired for the purpose.

Surely even the most self-confident and assured of artists must have moments of battling with self-doubt and so, in a way, every finished work of art is the triumph of one part of its creator's nature over another, and thus record of a Pyrrhic victory, gained and lost on the terribly personal battleground of one's own brainpan.

So if the little woman thinks you are capable of anything, and everything—well, you may not respect her intelligence, but when it comes to the old tussle with that inner devil, Doubt, she does help. After all she *might* be right. For once.

It took Irvin a long time to make up his mind. He was not a gambler. He was a man with an almost torturing sense of responsibility toward his family. He had seen what happens to families when the heads of them fail. He was now the highest-priced newspaperman in New York, which means the world. He had achieved security. Modest, and simple, but all the same security. He had very little saved; after all, he entirely supported five grown people and a child in the manner to which he was gradually accustoming them. God knows how long it would be before he could count on a steady sale of his work. Or indeed any sale at all. And his margin of money, therefore of time, was thus desperately limited.

So he stewed and he fretted and he worried and longed, and hoped and doubted. And walked, a million miles or so, up and down, twisting and twisting the buttons on his vest. That was the sign of strain. When one had to sew and sew and sew again the buttons back on Irvin's vest, and around them appeared a perfectly slick, shiny circle of cloth worn napless by his unconscious incessant gesture—he was worried.

Then Laura found an ally—Sam Blythe—who was running his famous political column in the *Saturday Evening Post* and was a great friend of its editor, George Horace Lorimer. Sam thought Irvin could write fiction, paying fiction too, and had interested Mr. Lorimer in the possibility.

So one summer, Irvin, driven by the two of them, worked out a compromise. He would ask for six weeks' vacation from the paper, we would go away with the Blythes to Lake Champlain and he'd try to write a short story.

The Blythes took a cottage on the lake, we a smaller one hard by, and everybody anticipated a pleasant and constructive vacation. It ended up by Irvin and Mr. Blythe abandoning almost all pursuits except that of watching out for their mail, by which they both set considerable store.

The very first day there the two of them had gone together down to the local post office to register their names and addresses, and there they made the acquaintance of the gentleman employed by the authorities to distribute the mail around that part of the lake. He was not a regular mail carrier, more a living concession to the laziness of summer visitors spoiled by city living, who preferred not having to walk anywhere from three to seven miles a day for their letters. This person was possessed of certain peculiarities which were instantly visible—for instance he had no more forehead than a Tennessee shad, and was wearing, on a blistering hot July day, a complete suit of black oilcloth. Later, but not much later, it became evident that his cranium and his clothes were not the only peculiar things about him.

"We've taken cottages here," explained Mr. Blythe. "Arrived last night and are planning to stay until September. My name is Blythe—Samuel Blythe—and this is Mr. Irvin Cobb."

"Do say?" was the answer, and then brightly: "Blythe? . . . Cobb? . . . Spell 'em both the same?"

Later when Dad and Mr. Blythe tactfully inquired of one of the village elders if this were not an odd sort of letter carrier, they were told that no, he wasn't at all odd, he was only the local half-wit. The township had arranged that he hold his present position so that the expense of his keep "won't come on the county."

For the rest of that summer Irvin never suffered a dull moment. He was too busy "waitin' for the evenin' mail."

In between times he wrote his story. Of this he announced that if it sold, well and good. That would at least prove whether or not he could write fiction, as of this stage in his development. If it did not sell he wished to hear no more on the subject.

He wrote "The Escape of Mr. Trimm." It was bought, at once, by Lorimer. Mr. Trimm for a character in a short story has had a good long life. For well over thirty years he has lived in anthologies, in courses of short-story writing, in reprints and in "selected readings."

But, said Irvin, hedging, one swallow does not a summer make, no one story in the *Post* a living for a large family.

So he hung onto his job, but began using his spare time, and heaven knows where he found any, to write short stories, until at last, as every one he wrote was bought, and Lorimer, like

Oliver Twist, kept asking for more, he felt justified in abandoning a steady weekly pay check.

He told me that when the first week rolled by, and payday
came, though not for him, he went near crazy. He could concentrate on nothing; he just stayed near a telephone, so that if
the pressure grew unbearable he might call the *World* at any
moment, and ask them to take him back. And twiddled two
sets of buttons off his vest.

Perhaps Mr. Lorimer knew this; at any rate he fixed up an
expedition that not only relieved the financial anxiety, for several months at least, but provided, for both Laura and Irvin,
the realization of one of their wildest dreams. He sent them
to Europe. Dad was to write for the *Post* a series of very highly
paid articles on his travels. His expenses were paid besides,
and Laura went for the ride.

Collected later, his articles made a little book and a big hit.
It was called *Europe Revised*.

Laura says that when she read it she was flabbergasted. She
had been with him every step of the way, she had seen everything he had seen. But had she? Evidently not. As she read
she decided that it must have been some other girl.

Also she said that he left out the funniest thing, and that was
the spectacle of herself and Irvin pretending to be sophisticated,
casual, take-it-in-your-stride tourists, when all the time they
were not only green as grass but scared limber besides.

"The time he insisted on going down to the dining room of
the Savoy in London for his breakfast, and the shocked incre-
dulity of the "chars" who were scrubbing it! . . . The time he
tangled with his first French telephone! Oh, my! . . . We
were *such* hicks."

His own account of this particular experience differs greatly
from her version, and grew to be one of his favorite anecdotes,

much polished with loving care through the years, a real "set piece" such as all storytellers eventually provide themselves with, entirely to their own satisfaction, although the most loving of families sometimes run out and bay the moon when, once again, Pa is set to tell *that* one.

He liked it so much that he wrote it down. I asked Laura if there was a word of truth in it, and she said, yes . . . a word. He *did* talk to somebody, by mistake, one late afternoon in the Hôtel Lotti in September 1913, and the place was certainly Paris (France). The rest of it she cannot guarantee. This is his version.

It had never occurred to me that I might have the psychic gift. If I thought about the matter at all I thought of it as one having an appeal to persons who are slenderer than I am. . . . For example, I could fancy Madame Sarah Bernhardt being psychic but I could not conceive of former President Taft in the rôle. In other words it did not seem probable that one could successfully be psychic by the pound. . . .

[My editing. He here explains how and why they were at the Hôtel Lotti. E. C.]

At the time we were not aware that this hotel was a favorite stopping-place for members of the nobility, and even of royalty when desiring privacy and quiet. . . . As it turned out, its guests then included the King of Greece, an Italian princess who featured her own private gold toothpick in the main dining-room at every meal, a Russian grand duke and a certain distinguished Englishwoman who bore a famous title and who was well known on both sides of the Atlantic. . . .

[Let us no longer stay coy. The lady was Lady Randolph Churchill, that same Jennie Jerome who married a younger son of the Duke of Marlborough and had a son called Winston. E. C.]

We reached Paris on a Saturday evening. That night we took in the life of the Boulevards, or as much of it as we could take in between eight o'clock and midnight.

I asked Laura at this point whether they attempted to "take in" the night life of Paris between eight o'clock and midnight out of innocence—or did Irvin get sleepy? She says he got sleepy. To continue with his account:

Next morning we saw the after-church parade of fashionable folk and rode through the Bois and in the afternoon went to the races at Longchamps.

[Shades of Marcel Proust and *Nana!* I wonder what they would have thought of the boy from Paducah? I know darn well what he thought of them! E. C.]

In the evening we were going to a theater and so, late in the afternoon, being pretty well fagged out, I went to my room to take a nap. Before lying down I drew the curtains to exclude the daylight but I made the mistake of not locking the outer door of my chamber. Presently I wakened out of a sound sleep to find that the lights had been flashed on and that a valet with a spade-shaped black beard was bending over the footboard of my bed and inquiring if there was anything he could do for Monsieur. I told him, yes there was; he could go and get a shave. . . .

Then the telephone, which stood on a tabouret in a corner of the room, began to emit curious sounds. It did not exactly ring, but it clicked and squeaked and gave off muffled, jingling notes as though it might be getting ready to ring. It was a French telephone and therefore was intended more for ornamentation than for utilitarian purposes. . . .

So when my telephone began to stutter I turned upon it a dubious eye. "Surely," said I to myself, "surely that kindly destiny which rules our lives will not call upon me to try to speak . . . with somebody who probably speaks nothing but French. I have lost my beauty-sleep, but I wish to keep what remains of my once sunny disposition." Just as I was saying that to myself the telephone quit rehearsing and rang intermittently. . . .

I lay there hoping that the instrument would presently cure itself of what ailed it, but no, the ringing kept on. It became

practically continuous. The clamor filled the room. So, finally I got up and I fitted the combination speaking-and-listening apparatus about my neck . . . and I said, somewhat shortly:

"Well, what is it?"

Over the wire came a voice saying in English:

"Are you there?"

"No," I said, "I'm here."

"Quite so," said the voice. "You're there. Who is it wants Lady Churchill?" (In his original she is called Lady Up-church, which is a very neat twist to the name.)

Taken though I was by surprise, I nevertheless rallied promptly.

"Well," I said, "I don't, for one."

The tone of the reply betokened a querulous insistence. . . .

"What! You don't want Lady Churchill?"

"Well," I said, "if you're going to make an issue of it I might take the proposition under consideration. When did Her Ladyship start doing this sort of thing?"

The shock was such that my unseen interrogator forgot to ring off and evidently was too grievously stricken to make any direct response. But over the wire I could hear that voice murmuring to its dazed owner these words.

"Oh, God bless my soul! What a frightful bounder! What a frightful Yankee bounder! Oh, God bless my soul!"

Now here comes the really significant and, from an occult standpoint, the interesting phase of the occurrence. At the very instant when the person at the other end of the wire spoke for the first time . . . I, standing there alone in my room, had visualized him. The inflection in his voice and the depth of tone told me it must be a man. The accent unmistakably had been that of an educated Englishman. But it was more than the vague figure of an Englishman that flashed before my vision. I saw him plainly revealed as a small and narrow-shouldered person in dark clothes, having the look about him, moreover, of being somebody's social secretary. . . . I saw that he had large and prominent front teeth and a pair of those outspreading, translucent ears, and I somehow knew that when he stood in the bright sunlight the rays of the sun would percolate through his ears as through the stained-glass windows of a memorial chapel. . . . I saw that customarily his mouth hung slightly ajar because of the presence of adenoids—not the small, domestic adenoids which we know in America, but the large fruity golden-russet adenoids of old England. . . . I saw that his trousers were a wee bit short for him in the legs and that the collar of his coat stood well away from his neck. In a flash I saw all this.

Now then, for the sequel: Two days later at the door of the hotel I, going out, narrowly escaped bumping into a person coming in. In every regard this person was the physical embodiment of the conjured image of that Sunday afternoon. . . . I addressed the proprietor of the hotel. . . .

"That gentleman yonder," I said, "who is he?"

"I do not know ze gentleman's name," he said, "but he is ze private secretary of Lady Churchill." [He] drew nearer to me and discreetly sank his voice to a conversational undertone: "I do not know why it is," he said, "but always ze private secretaries of rich English ladies look like zat one."

Am I psychic or am I not?

[Later on, in London during the First World War, he met Lady Randolph, and told her the story. She laughed her head off.]

Quite innocently Laura came near to spoiling the trip for him by developing a mad passion for caviar. Every night at dinner she'd wave away the proffered menu. "I'll just have caviar . . . and whatever you order, dear."

She noticed that he kept growing gloomier and gloomier, and to save her, couldn't imagine why until at last one night, over her caviar, she burst into tears. She could not stand it! He was so cross, and so dour, all the time nowadays. He was spoiling her trip. What in the world was the matter?

"It's that caviar," he said. "You're bankrupting me."

"What on earth are you talking about?" she demanded. "You can't sit there and tell me these little old fish eggs are *expensive,* can you?"

After that she varied her diet a bit, and they both began to enjoy themselves, and as a reward for being a good girl and refraining from eating them into the poorhouse, where, as he pointed out, caviar is so seldom served, he bought her a beautiful dress in Paris. The first Mrs. Arnold Bennett, who was a Frenchwoman, helped her pick it out. It was at this time that I inherited that green and white job.

It was nice of Mrs. Bennett to take Laura under her wing, because Irvin was nursing a smoldering resentment against Arnold. For years, with the greatest relish, he used to repeat what Oliver Herford said about Bennett's work, and although it is a profound remark and one to be taken to the heart and there cherished, I am sure that Dad would not have loved it quite so much if it had been said of any other writer. He and Mr. Herford had been discussing contemporary English writers and Dad asked what, if any, was his friend's opinion of the chronicler of the Midlands.

"To tell you the truth, Irvin," said Mr. Herford, "something I wrote once, in a critical way, concerning Arnold Bennett, so prejudiced me against the man that I never could bear to read a word he wrote."

And why did he nourish this grudge, and nurture it and keep it green? For a strange reason, or so it seems to me, who like most women don't get mad at just the same things that men do. Such queer reasons they dig up!

Certainly if Arnold Bennett had committed a hideous crime there could hardly have been more outcry against him, not only from Irvin, but from most of the large company who witnessed his horrible deed, which consisted in his refusing a helping of terrapin stew at a luncheon given for him by Mr. Lorimer!

Thirty years later Irvin's eyes would kindle with a righteous wrath as he told about it. "Lorimer had sent especially for the terrapin. Sent a man south to pick them out himself! They were cooked in the finest madeira! It was the best damned terrapin anybody ever ate. And that—that buck-toothed, jimpy-jawed, underbred counterjumper of an ignorant Limey put on his spectacles, studied the dish, asked what it was, and when told said coldly, "Oh! Turtle? Well, I shan't touch it!" Just like that! Turned up his nose and no explanation, no nothing. Just wouldn't touch it! *He* wouldn't touch it! The so and so!"

It was later explained that Mr. Bennett suffered excruciatingly from stomach trouble and was doubled up in agonies if he ate any but the simplest and plainest of foods. No matter!

I verily believe that Irvin took such a very dim view of Lend-Lease to Great Britain thirty years later because Arnold Bennett refused to eat terrapin.

It was a year or so after this dastardly act on the part of the author of *The Old Wives' Tale* that Laura had a shock, and one that she never quite got over. She discovered that Irvin could make a fool of himself. This seemed to her an awful reversal of nature, like a cockeyed, upside-down miracle. If her wonderful, wise, infallible, *smart* Irvin could do anything so downright silly . . . why—why, the heavens might fall! . . . It would surprise her no more.

In other words she found out what a sucker he was.

Already every panhandler in New York knew that he was the easiest "touch" in the town, as she did of course, for he had never been so poor as to pass a beggar without leaving a contribution behind him. He always looked a little sheepish when performing this act, and was quick to explain that someday he might hit somebody who really was hungry, and did not want to take any chances. My personal opinion is that he was abjectly superstitious. Well, it's not what you'd call an ugly superstition, is it?

When we were living on Park Avenue in the nineteen twenties he had a rather revealing little shock directly stemming from this ritualistic placating of the implacable god Luck. I was present and witnessed the reaction which was highly revelatory. We had come home together one afternoon and as we were going up to his apartment the elevator boy handed him a letter that had been left there earlier by the writer in person. Dad ripped it open and read it immediately. It stated that the writer, although unknown to Mr. Cobb, had been referred to him by his old and good and intimate friend Warden Lawes of Sing Sing, a man always willing to help an ex-convict who was sincerely trying to buck a suspicious tough new world. And both he and the undersigned would be infinitely grateful for any help from Mr. Cobb ... any help at all, but a hundred dollars would be nice.

"It's a touch," said Dad. "And a crude one at that."

"I don't know about that," I said. "Seems to me it's a pretty clever letter."

"Oh, it's that all right," he agreed. "But there's one big mistake in it. That's why I say it's crude. You see the writer is recommended by my dear and good old friend Warden Lawes. And it just so happens that I don't know Warden Lawes."

"What are you going to do about it? Give him the hundred anyhow?"

"Certainly not! Don't be so silly. . . . I—I'll make it ten. . . . Or maybe fifteen."

He went on up to his room, but a few seconds later called out to me to know if I happened to have twenty dollars in my purse, as he'd like to borrow it until tomorrow. I said I was sorry but did not have that much on me and he muttered something that sounded like, "Where in hell is my checkbook. . . . Oh! . . . O.K. I've found it . . ." and retreated again.

At that moment the phone rang and I answered it and asked if I might take the message, as I was Mr. Cobb's daughter and he was occupied. After some hesitation the caller agreed to give it to me. I was to tell my father than a very well-known con man had been arrested that afternoon, and was now in jail. This was Sergeant So-and-So—he was calling Mr. Cobb because among the personal belongings taken from the man at the station house was a notebook filled with names and addresses and labeled "Sucker List A."

"Was my father's name on the list?" I asked.

"Was it on it! Say, lady, it was the very first one! And with four stars!"

I went upstairs and knocked. "Look, darling," I said. "Tear up that check. You've missed your opportunity. You're too late. The guy's in jail."

He opened his door and I told him of my conversation with the gendarmerie.

"So he had my name on his list, did he?" he asked.

"Listen, Abou Ben Irvin," I said. "It led all the rest!"

He got very red in the face and began to scuffle around among the papers on his desk. "Looks like I ought to stop being such a fool, doesn't it?" he asked.

"Looks that way."

He gave me a glowering glance, then grinned reluctantly. "I won't say it isn't kind of a shock to find out what an easy mark I am," he said. "But dammit, Buff, there must be *somebody* else who hasn't got any more savvy than I have. Why, I haven't talent enough, much less money enough, to be the *biggest* sucker in the city of New York!" However, if he was a sucker, it was because he chose to be, not because he was fooled—much.

I remember how, on yet another occasion when we had been for a walk and were returning home together, we were stopped at our corner by a rat-faced little man who confided to us in a whisper that he could sell us a wonderful bargain in furs, that is, if we would buy them quick, right there, and (sinking his voice), ask no questions. It's an old, old racket, I'm told. The sucker thinks the furs are stolen, of course. They aren't. They are merely very bad furs for which one pays a good price in anticipation of a larcenous bargain. That's another axiom of the trade: The best suckers are never averse to a little law-breaking, not if it can be done anonymously.

Dad was most affable. "My dear," said he to me, "would you like some furs? If so, we will go upstairs and I will buy you some."

The man demurred; he couldn't see his way clear to going upstairs at the moment. That was too bad, Dad said, for unless he consented to come up, how was he to be paid?

Rat-face then suggested that the gentleman send the money down, if he didn't happen to have it on him.

"Money?" asked Dad. "Who said anything about money? You don't expect to be paid in genuine writ of the mint money, do you?"

"Certainly I expect to be paid in money. . . . What the—! What were you planning to pay me in?"

"Why, I expected to make a sort of swap," said Dad. "Your furs for my gold brick—the one I inherited from an uncle. My uncle paid a great deal of money for that gold brick. It's as handsome a gold bri——"

But the little man was backing away from us as fast as he could—backing, mind you, with the strangest expression on his face. He looked a bit as though he had just been kicked in the stomach. Suddenly he snarled, "Say, you sound to me like one big fool!" And then ran just as hard as he could.

Dad chuckled to himself all the way upstairs. Just the same, if you made him mad, he could be deadly. As he said of his beloved Will Hogg, he was not a man to prank with. There was the time that he spent six months recovering an overcharge of thirty-five cents on a checked trunk, driving the entire personnel of the Santa Fe Railroad nuts until he got it returned to him, from the president's own august hand, I believe, and the time that he tangled with the surly taxi driver and . . .

But perhaps that is a tale deserving of a full treatment. We had been to the theater one night, and returned in a cab driven by a gentleman who scared us limp with the speed and recklessness of his driving. He seemed to be enjoying a bet with himself; if he got us home sound in mind and limb, he'd lose that round. Even in his more tranquil moments, as when forced to stop by a congestion of traffic, which was all that did make him stop, no mere traffic light daunting him, let me tell you, he then jerked the cab so badly that Moie and I were continually being hurled off the seat to the floor and even Dad, ever a stolid, not to say, massive sitter, several times found himself inadvertently kneeling as though to pray. But long before we reached home we all agreed that in our present situation prayer was what we were standing in need of—standing, sitting, sliding and bounding in need of——

Finally, and surely with the aid of angels, we arrived safely, and Dad, giving thanks, was reaching in his pocket for his money when he looked again at the meter and realized that it registered sixty cents more than he had paid for the same trip just three hours before.

"Your meter's wrong," he said, mildly enough, with his money ready in his hand. "Better have it seen to."

The driver then gave a piercing scream, descended from his seat in a highly belligerent manner and demanded his money, and no more back talk.

At that Dad returned his change to his pocket and said he was beginning to see this thing in a different light, and how about the man's giving him his number, so that the question of that sixty cents might be taken up with his company. "For somehow," said Dad, elevating his cigar and pulling at his hat, "a feeling is beginning to steal over me—a feeling that I am not going to pay that sixty cents, after all."

From then on things worked up into quite a lively little fracas, with our doorman and a couple of interested passers-by getting involved, and was interrupted only by the arrival of a very large and bored Irish cop. Bored, as he later explained, because such arguments were forever being started, but as for finishing them—— Well, that was a different matter now! You see, that would require an appearance at the traffic court early in the morning. Very early. And many and many were the outraged citizens who breathed vengeance and fury at midnight, who yet found their longing for justice strangely dimmed at six-thirty of a cold and wintry day.

Now if Mr. Cobb, for instance, should insist on preferring charges against this man, it would mean that the cop must appear at court the next morning, and this after a long cold night's work, mind you, at the time he was needing his breakfast and his sleep. Then, if Mr. Cobb changed his mind and did not appear, after all—and here he wearily shrugged—why, his hard-earned rest would be sacrificed to no purpose.

"Don't worry," said Dad. "I will be there." And he was. And they found that the taxi driver was a paroled convict, not eligible to hold a license as a public conveyor, who was then promptly found guilty of having a crooked meter and half a dozen other little matters, including bootlegging, and as promptly returned to Sing Sing to serve out his original sentence, with a bit added.

Well and good. So was justice served. Only the taxi driver left behind him a wife and a parcel of kids, now destitute. They appealed to Dad. And from then on he sent them a check every month until their father and husband was once again restored to society and the bosom of his family, a bosom not so tender as he had anticipated it might be, perhaps, for by this time they seemed to feel that as good providers went, Irvin Cobb was a lot more reliable, not to say regular and generous, than their own dear daddy. Indeed they said that for all of them, why, Pops could stay in the hoosegow for the rest of his natural life. Or, on second thought, the rest of Mr. Cobb's natural life.

Dad figured that this little affair must have cost him several thousand dollars. But he did not care. He was perfectly satisfied. Nobody who drove a taxi that badly could gyp him out of sixty cents. He was not a man to be pranked with.

So, you see, when we told the story of the ex-convict with the sucker list to Laura, she was not a bit surprised. "Why, of course," she said. "I only wonder we don't have hundreds of experiences like that. Remember the time you bought the pecan grove?"

"Now, Loll," said Dad, "what's the use in dragging in all that ancient history? I bought it. And I'm sorry. And I do not care to hear any more about it."

"But I do," I said. "How come? Nobody ever told me we owned a pecan grove. Tell me about it."

So Laura did, after Dad had left the room, closing the door with some firmness behind him.

Mr. Lorimer had sent Irvin out to the West Coast to do a follow-up on *Europe Revised,* and she, getting very de luxe, had sublet a little apartment in town for the time that he would be gone. No sooner was she settled than an old gentleman, claiming to be a boyhood friend of her father, came a-calling. But his visit was not purely social. Oh, no! Mixed with the delicious reminiscences of better times in Liberty County, Georgia, another and more practical theme kept weaving itself in and out of the conversation. Somehow they always got back to the advantages of owning a pecan grove. And oddly enough he had one to sell. Laura managed to get rid of the old man two or three hundred times, without committing herself to becoming the Little Lady of the Big Nuts, but things had come to such a pass and so persistent was Papa's pal that she no longer used the front elevator but preferred leaving by the back entrance. Could be, someday, she'd be whisked into the garbage-disposal wagon . . . just the same she'd arrive at the dump a free woman—and no pecan grower.

The first morning that Irvin came back from his trip, heavy-laden with gifts and anecdote, he was just settling down to tell all, and enjoy hot waffles and a good listener, when old Pa Pecan came bumbling by again, announced from downstairs by a smart bellboy.

"Oh, bother!" said Laura. "Here's that old nuisance! Wouldn't you know he'd turn up your very first morning home!"

"What old nuisance?"

"Papa's friend. The one who wants to sell us a pecan grove."

"Now, Laura! You haven't bought a pecan grove? . . . There's a woman for you! . . . Leave her for six weeks—and she bankrupts you."

"Certainly I haven't bought a pecan grove. I've only been driven half crazy getting away from the old man."

"Let him come up," said Irvin grandly. "I will tend to him. And afterward we will hear no more of this nonsense."

"Now, Irvin . . . it is much easier just to say we are out."

"Easier perhaps. For today. And tomorrow he will be back."

"He certainly will!"

"Very well. I will see him now. And get the whole thing over with. . . . Once and for all. You had better leave us alone. You're such a softy."

"All right," said Laura. "I'll go in the bedroom. You see him alone. And say *No*."

The doorbell rang and she started for her room, turning back but once.

"You won't buy a pecan grove, now, will you, Irvin? Papa says they *never* pay. And . . ."

"Really, Laura," said Irvin, "do you think that I have lost the last remnants of my sanity? There are a few things that I know that we don't need. . . . Seven toes, for instance . . . or a pecan grove! You just leave everything to me!"

Well, the visit was not of long duration. The old pest was

in and out quicker than she had ever been able to maneuve
him. There was no question about it. Irvin was wonderful
He was also the owner of a pecan grove.

We used to receive a big bag of nuts from our property every
Christmas without fail. In return for this all we had to do
was pay the taxes and the upkeep and the assessments. That'
when she began pressing him to give all his money to tha
nice man at the bank to look after. Somehow . . . "You see
darling," she'd say, "it will save you such a lot of trouble. And
such a lot of money!"

Chapter 4

A LONG RIDE DOWN EASY STREET

WE had taken the regular steps, first to the funny little apartment, then out to the suburbs, now we took the third and returned to town—to a big comfortable apartment on Riverside Drive. In those days it was not quite as inevitable that those coming up in the world should live on the East Side. Now, of course, the East Side is a mania and the way my smart (or you might say "smarty" or even "smarty-panty") friends carry on, you'd think that domiciling oneself anywhere west of Fifth Avenue meant exposure to all sorts of horrible privations, even dangers—like going of one's own free will into a leper colony. . . . Of course one can lunch at Jack and Charlie's without running much risk, there having been only two or three cases of tsetse-fly fever picked up on West Fifty-second Street, but into the hinterland beyond "21" and it is necessary to carry bottled water, and beads with which to trade with the natives. On a really long safari, say up to the headwaters on One Hundred and Tenth Street where we used to live, one takes one's own goats and avoids the pigmies and the cannibal tribes.

But we weren't studying on chic then—and probably the word had not yet invaded our vocabularies—and in our innocence we thought we were very "swanky," which means the same thing, in our nice big apartment, which had such a fine view of the river and the Palisades across the way. There was a great ease coming into our lives; we were getting more than comfortable now, we were getting extravagant.

We set up a car that winter, one of those enormous old Pierce-Arrows, an open job with the headlights mounted on the running boards like a bug's eyes. Remember? Laura had a special costume for taking drives, which we did every day. Not going anywhere—just taking a drive. And what drives! There weren't any parkways; one was trundled for hours through mean, dingy streets until at last one reached the country, and then it was always time to turn around and come home.

Lots of people did this. I remember that most afternoons just at the time that we set forth so did a nice old lady and gentleman who lived in our building. It got so that we missed them if they didn't turn up.

Their car was a limousine upholstered in flowered chintz, with little ruffled curtains at the windows, including the one the chauffeur looked out of. Now these were two very fragile old parties, obviously of a high degree of respectability, but when they teetered into that chintz bower-on-wheels they did look a little bit like they were going to bed.

Downtown we used to see large numbers of lavender-colored cars, and blue and pink and white ones. These were either very open, or very closed indeed, and usually had a languid dog, a dog with no honest trade as Dad used to say, sitting up by the driver and a pretty lady sitting alone in the back. Laura turned her nose up at these equipages but I thought they were lovely. When I grew up I too was going to have a shiny white car and a borzoi dog.

And that, come to think of it, is not a bad idea. You get so tired of the eternal modern blacks and grays and dark blues, and although my heart no longer craves a borzoi, those sorrowful inchworms on stilts, I know a French poodle intimately, her name being Little Miss of Stagwell (she's a Queenstown, Maryland, girl; her folks were refugees) but who answers indiscriminately to Missy or Miss Kiss or Miss Cake or the Daisy Dog or You Fool Pup, and she would certainly like a pale pink open car—and very becoming it would be to her too!

But enough! Let me return to 1914, and Miss Kiss not even thought of yet (although how we lived without her all those years!).

It was now that we took up the pleasant custom of going away for the week end—so do the times grow recognizably historic. I say "we," for those blessed innocents, my parents, always lugged me along with them. It's a mystery how they managed to put the bite on their friends like this, for certainly I must have been a sore trial to any hostess planning a gay and sophisticated little gathering, being an outsize, square-rigged, dark child forever alternating between attacks of the deepest gloom and convulsive fits of the giggles. I was also the most awkward of creatures, if one excepts a half-grown kangaroo.

Up at Mr. William Randolph Hearst's place—no, place is not the word—up at Mr. Hearst's barony, San Simeon, I once saw a hobbledehoy young buck of a kangaroo trying to back himself into his mama's pouch, but when, with great grunting and to-do, he had got part of his person arranged to his liking in mama's marsupial sack and was about to settle down and repose himself, he would notice that several yards of his anatomy had escaped from his old home and was dangling out in the wide-open spaces again. You could see that he was about to break down and cry from pure exasperation, and his mama wore an expression at once patient and fretful as one who would say, "Come now, Junior, you're getting to be a big boy now! See for yourself, if you won't take my word for it." How clearly that unhappy boy kangaroo's struggle brought back my own young self!

Ah me! I can remember the winter day when the family toted me along on a little expedition out to Margaret Illington's country place. Remember and writhe! We were provided with a wonderful picnic lunch, to be eaten before a big fire on Margaret's sun porch, and when lunchtime came I volunteered my help, which I still think they should have had enough sense to refuse, and was told to take myself into the pantry and carry out plates and glasses. I had made two or three successful trips, heavy-laden and very pleased at my own deftness, when my father happened to notice what I was up to. Then, "Good gracious, Margaret," said he, "don't let that child carry those pretty, expensive plates. She's bound and sure to break every one of them."

Being ever an easy weeper, the tears of humiliation sprang at once to my eyes, but I was determined that no one should see them, so in a sort of blind anguish I kept on with my task, saying to myself, "Yea, verily, though they scorn me, see how willingly and carefully and gracefully I am carrying their horrid old plates" . . . and walked smack into a large bird cage, home for a dozen or so canaries, and knocked it clean off the wall. And, oh, yes, in the ensuing confusion all the plates got broken.

To make everything just dandy for everybody, on such parties I also refused to "play." Visiting children were rounded up for my benefit at their peril. What I wanted to do, intended to do, did, was to glue myself to my papa as closely as possible, and listen to the company swap stories. After a few experiences with me the various hostesses realized that I was perfectly happy thus, and only thus, and after they got used to it I think they would forget that I was there, which was jake by me.

Only Dad would remember me occasionally, when he wanted to tell a naughty one, and then he would send me from the room. I always went without protest, and was pretty good about not trying to eavesdrop, but wept a little, privately.

Yes, that's the way those people used to amuse themselves; by telling stories. It seems pretty weird to me now, for all my pals are game addicts, or if not playing at something or other, they talk about things. Politics, movies, books, war, people, money, something. But not Dad's crowd. They told jokes. They set up lovely country houses, gave big parties, traveled about the land to visit each other, gathered on pleasant porches and told jokes.

As I remember none of them played games. George Doran was a golfer, but he was also a Canadian who had lived much in England, which explained his eccentricity in this regard.

There was a reason for this. They had all grown up before the great sport age dawned in the United States, when only the children of the rich were given the training and facilities for games. Dad said that when he was a boy, and not such a big boy either, there was literally nothing for the young crowd to do but to hang around poolrooms and saloons. Once, when he was about sixteen, some of the boys thought to play a little baseball in an empty lot, but were so greatly criticized—big oafs like that playing a game right out in public—that they never repeated the experiment. The village elders made considerable noise on this occasion, and it was generally held that at the best the boys had done an undignified and unbecoming thing, but some of the stricter folk thought this too mild a condemnation. Why, wasting time, which is money, was downright immoral, at least it was if your mother's pastor and family were good old-fashioned Presbyterians. Living in a firmly evangelical Protestant town in the horse-and-buggy days must have had its drawbacks. What I sometimes wonder is, did it have anything but drawbacks?

Well, that explains their not playing games, but not all those jokes.

"Well, you see," said Dad, "in my youth one did not talk politics and such at a party where ladies were present. You told them that you would not think of boring them. You told them not to bother their pretty little heads." He sighed. Maybe he was sighing because he was feeling a little frustrated, for he was never capable of carrying on a conversation with a woman. If he liked a girl, he told her selected stories. If he liked her very much, he permitted her to tell him one. It was about as awkward a way to make friends as any I can think of, except maybe employing a semaphore, but the only one at his command.

This habit was so strong that except he be very intimate with you or alone with you, or both, he never talked to, but always at you. At dinner parties he was always entirely silent, with a dark, penetrating silence reminiscent of Egyptian tombs, or else he would abruptly raise his voice, wait until he got everybody's attention, and then tell a story. After dinner it was his custom to rock about like an unhappy elephant until he had located a book, and he would then relapse into it with a grateful grunt. In his last years he used to say that parties tired him terribly because "nobody else does his share. It always seems to be up to me and I get just plumb tuckered out under the strain."

One of the few times that I can remember him joining in a general sort of give and take—give a little, take a lot—was when an inspired guest propounded this question: If you were possessed of a magic talisman which would fetch the dead back into the land of the living, what twelve people would be the most fun to ask for the week end?

There are endless possibilities to this peculiarly futile sort of imagining, as everyone who has ever tried it has soon discovered. We must have worked up a hundred lists in our time, though always with great din and outcry as somebody's pet particular ghost is always being eliminated or slighted, which hurts the feelings of his sponsor.

We also found that before we could really settle down to the guest list we always had to plan a new house for their reception, as we never owned a real one with enough bedrooms. You see, there can never be any doubling up at this house party, because no one has ever been known to ask a married couple. Think it over. If you can think of a single, solitary married couple out of all history, where the wife would be as welcome as the husband, or vice versa, I'd like to know about them. Antony and Cleopatra have been suggested. But that's cheating. Maybe they were married, in Egypt. But that's her story. Just the same, if one asked to see the little woman's wedding lines, I'll bet she'd get awfully flustered. And anyhow, who wants Antony—that great Roman booby?

Matter of fact, there are singularly few soldiers or dictators, with the possible exception of King David and Julius Caesar, that anyone would choose to spend twenty minutes with, much less a long Friday-till-Monday.

Dad was greatly taken with this game, but at last he grew bored with it and stopped it once and for all by saying, "**Oh,** shucks! I don't know what twelve I would ask. I only know the twelve I wouldn't."

"And who are they?"

"The twelve Apostles," said he.

Of course, his method of conversing would have been dreadful, intolerable even, if it had not been that he told stories, funny ones, dramatic ones and sad ones, better than anyone in this world. First place he was a great mimic. . . . Why, I've seen that man look more like a lobster than a lobster does and once when he was impersonating a moose I am quite sure that he would have fooled anyone except maybe another moose, and it a lady. Also his speech was more colorful, more vivid and saltier than his writing. He always had the unexpected, the fantastic word, at his tongue's end, and he was one of the few people I ever knew who, in this degenerate age, spoke in complete sentences. He never chopped off a phrase or forgot the verb or a predicate. This gave even an improvisation the finish of a conscious work of art. Still and all and nevertheless, when anybody else starts out by telling me that they have just heard a new story, which will slay me, I always beg them to go and hunt up someone else to slay—not that they ever do—because what with one thing and another I don't make a very good audience. Seems as though I had fallen into my anecdotage.

But of course it could be that I am spoiled. I knew the master.

But to get back a bit, life in the golden age—for that's what he always claimed those years before the First World War were—was interrupted for us, as it was for half the world and more, by the news that the German Army had invaded Belgium.

We were spending a few weeks up at a lake in Canada, and Dad has told me that when he realized the big fight was on, he was in a most unhappy and rebellious frame of mind. Of course, as an old newspaperman he was frantic to work on the greatest story of them all. The news, in those first days, was to him like the trumpet which sayeth Ha! and he like an old war horse who sniffs gunpowder from afar. Short-story writer, was he? Special-feature concocter, eh? Deviser of pale little plots and author of pastiches, songs and funny sayings? He was like hell! He was a newspaperman. And he wasn't going to get to go to the big show!

Then that blessed George Horace Lorimer sent a wire—and he was to go after all. As correspondent for the *Saturday Evening Post*. It was a good thing that Mr. Lorimer dreamed up this assignment. If he had not, I think poor Dad would have literally swelled up and gone pop. Following that assignment he lived through a terrific personal adventure and the pieces he wrote from Belgium and Germany made him a nationally known figure. From then on his career was pretty well guaranteed; he could sell anything that he wrote at fancy prices; he had caught the wave, and was to roll along on top of it for a long time.

Once, as told here earlier, an inspiration came to him, and by following it he got his first job in New York. Now there came a time when he was in Germany and in jail, or but recently released from it, and he and three other correspondents were going nuts from frustration, and he remembered that old dodge with the letter, and used it again. Those who were with him say that the whole thing was so incredible that they suddenly looked upon him with a sort of awe as the players in *Green Pastures* did when "de Lawd rar' back and pass a miracle."

The following account is his:

We were many miles from Berlin, with no means of getting there. We had been in custody and still were under suspicion. [They were indeed, having been arrested outside of Brussels while merrily following the German Army in its advance on Paris, being provided at the time with no means of identification whatsoever. Naturally they told their captors, with considerable emphasis, that they were Americans, but they had no way to prove this . . . though having bought their going-to-war clothes in London, their coats were decked out with English tailors' tabs, which gave their names but hardly supported their claims of being unfortunate war-trapped neutrals. They came very near getting shot as spies.] There were resident correspondents in Berlin who knew the heads of the German Government. . . . It was natural to suppose that to them would come the coveted opportunity to go to the front. . . .

We grew more and more desperate. Every day the face of

war was shifting; any hour the selected correspondents might be starting under military escort for the battle lines; any hour after that the rule of absolute exclusion for our kind might be revived.

It was then that Irvin came up with the idea of writing a letter. It was not so flippant as that one he had sent to the editor of the *Sun;* it surpassed flipness and approached audacity, nay, touched lese majesty. For it was addressed, as man to man, to the German Kaiser in person.

They consulted a wealthy German manufacturer who had befriended them in Aix-la-Chapelle, also asking him to word the request in the proper forms. Dad writes:

Well, when he had rallied somewhat he told us in strained and startled tones that what we desired was impossible, preposterous, unheard of. It just naturally wasn't done, and that was all there was to it.

"Why," he said, "you gentlemen do not know the court etiquette in such matters as these; you do not even know the proper language in which to address His Majesty."

"Quite right," the spokesman for our trio answered. . . . "[But] you have told us before now that your emperor is a great business man. And that is exactly what we mean to write—a business letter. . . . And now the question is, will you undertake to start that letter forward by wire through the proper channels after we write it?"

This second shock to his Prussian sensibilities seemed almost as severe as the first one had been. Having somewhat recovered, he warned us that the entire machinery of officialdom would stand as a stone wall between us and the impiety we contemplated."

But they wore down his powers of resistance, he quit expostulating finally and gave his reluctant consent to aid them, but disclaimed any responsibility for the possible consequences of their madness. Indeed he hoped, as a sincere friend, that they *might* be put down as mad, thus escaping the punishment, such as the descent of a bolt of lightning from an outraged heaven, which would surely befall them if they were judged sane.

So we went away and in conference drafted our letter—a plain business letter setting forth a plain business proposition; a letter not too formal, and yet, I trust, not too chatty. When it had been translated into German we took it back to our unhappy legate.

On reading it he suffered Shock III. Nevertheless, being a man of his word, he took it and prepared to start it upon its way. He then bade us good night in a voice which seemed to indicate he did not expect to see us soon again, if at all. His attitude was one of unspoken sympathy for three comparatively harmless lunatics who shortly would vanish out of his life forevermore.

We sat down to wait. We waited three days. On the morning of the fourth day came a gorgeous military figure, wrapped in a magnificent long gray coat, with medals on his chest and the badges of a staff colonel on his uniform. He bore to us an imposing parchment document, heavy with seals and ribbons, on which, in German script, was a statement, a proclamation, informing all whom it might concern—and, as it turned out, it seemed deeply to concern everybody in the German army, from field marshals down, who had the inestimable privilege of reading it—that . . . we three . . . might go pretty much where we pleased in and about the German battle lines, might have the exclusive use of a military automobile . . . might make notes, carry cameras, and take photographs, might commandeer food and tires and gasoline and billets, might bear arms for our own defense—might do, in fact, almost anything we pleased so long as we . . . respected the customary restrictions. And it was signed by the Kaiser in his own fair hand.

Now Irvin was a highly sensitive and imaginative man and

war did things to him as it does to all men, even the stupidest or the steadiest . . . and this, as far as his nerves were concerned, I think that he had never been. There had been too much pressure put upon him when he was too young, and both too highly strung and held on too tight a rein—or perhaps it was that he had never had the time to seek, or find, any real inner poise.

But one thing there was that brought healing and peace into the house of his spirit, and that was a good long hard trip in the woods. His own ego stopped hunting him when he was hunting something himself, and when he was fishing for fish he was let off fishing for the answers. As he grew older this passion, for it was just that, for solitude and the chase grew stronger, not weaker. One of the last things he wrote was the following ecstatic paean of purple praise, which he called "A Fisherman's Paradise." I think that he made a conscious effort to dye his typewriter keys in the same blazing colors that stain the canyon walls of his earthly heaven. To be less highfalutin about it, he was simply nuts about the place.

"All my life, seems to me, I've been hearing of the thing called a Fisherman's Paradise. When I was a boy I read about it. After I grew up, having caught the disease of being a fisherman, which is a very pleasant disease and takes one to far and pleasant places but is incurable, I went looking for it, hither and yon.

During my questings I had many small adventures and saw many sights and met many agreeable fellows who likewise were seeking this Fisherman's Paradise, and from time to time I caught my share of lusty fish. But I couldn't spy out that Angler's Heaven; couldn't find that Celestial City of the piscicapturist, with its finned angels and its scaled cherubim and its saints with gills on 'em. It was guaranteed in the advertisements, it was mentioned in the travel books, it was pictured by the tourist agents, but somehow it eluded me as it likewise had eluded so many of my brother Waltonians.

Either by intent or by haphazard, I have happened more than once upon a Fisherman's Hell, made so by skeeters or by black flies or by both. I have gloomed and mourned in a Fisherman's Purgatory where proper fish abounded but by reason of weather conditions or water conditions or just the sheer perversity of the creatures themselves, could not be induced to strike. For better identification I might add that your typical Fisherman's Purgatory is a scape of water in which the fish bit freely last week and with an ever greater freedom are confidently expected to be biting next week, but this week—no, positively no, absolutely no, —— the —— luck to—*no!*

There are men who long ago would have ceased to seek this Realm of the Ichthyologically Blest; men who would have lost heart and thenceforth been content to flitter their flies across ordinary brooks, always dreaming of the unattainable Kingdom but resigned to the knowledge that they never would view its beatitudes nor yet partake of its perfections.

But I kept on searching, north, south, east and west. And so at length I came upon that for which so long I had sought. Up in the huddled midst of the Canadian Rockies I came upon Maligne Lake. It was on my birthday—thus did the Fates decree—that I came upon it. Past fifty, the man who celebrates his birthday is either a romantic or else he's just a plain ass. But with psalms of thanksgiving and loud cries of joy, singing with a hey-niddy-noddy and a fol-de-rol-day and whatever else is suitable to sing with under the circumstances, I celebrated the birthday, not because it was a birthday of mine but because upon it I first saw Maligne Lake.

It is very easy for us to grow extravagant when telling of a thing which deeply has excited our admiration. So I shall restrain myself. I shall not be exuberant. I shall not even permit myself to speak enthusiastically of this matter. Calmly, dispassionately, conservatively, almost listlessly, I merely say that from the standpoint of beauty and the standpoint of fishability and from all the other standpoints I can think of off-hand, Maligne Lake, up yonder in Jasper National Park, is the most beautiful lake and the most fishable lake that ever was on this planet or, I reckon, ever will be while the stars hold to their courses and the speckled trout comes to the lure.

From all accounts Maligne Lake must have been the last great scenic marvel on this continent to be discovered by articulate humans, barring only Rainbow Bridge, and by an interesting coincidence both were first beheld—by Caucasians at least —in the same year. In an adjacent chapter I propose to endeavor to deal with Rainbow Bridge according to its merits.

Before 1909, no white person's eyes, so far as the records show, ever rested upon Maligne Lake in its almost incredible loveliness. So, alongside of Yellowstone and Glacier and Mammoth Cave and Niagara and Yosemite and California's Big Trees and Gaspé and Chapultepec and Mount Misti and the rest of them, it's practically a babe in arms. For centuries after most of the New World's wonders had been explored— and exploited—Maligne Lake, unnamed, uncharted, unplumbed, yea, unsuspected, was declaring its glories only to the skies and the peaks, to the wild goats and the skirmishing bighorn sheep. Some wandering Indian trailers, following once after a caribou herd, climbed over a rampart half a mile high and, stricken to numbed silence, gazed down upon it. And then they took their moccasined feet in their hands and they went right on away from those parts without waiting for supper or anything. Its mystery daunted their simple aborigine souls. Its sheer majesty affrighted them. Its unique setting was to them a thing unutterable and more than unutterable, unearthly, which indeed it is. So they pulled their freight out of there and dusted hell-for-leather down the Divide to the flatlands, and after a spell began once more breathing regularly. But they talked of what they had beheld and the talk fell on the eardrums of certain civilized hearers who, being so-called

Nordics, caught fire with the unslakable fever of curiosity which is of their breed, and these parties turned pathfinders, and eventually, after many disappointments and at least three fruitless efforts, solved the secret of its hiding place and told it to the world. That though is another story and should be told, but in its own place.

For me the job is comparatively simple. All I have to do is to describe for you a spot so filled up with grandeur and grandness as to be beyond description. . . . Well, now that that little undertaking is, thank goodness, over and done with, I'm aiming to fill in a few odd corners of the canvas with incidental brush strokes bringing mention of some of the details:

When Maligne Lake was foaled from the womb of Creation —and it must have been a noisy borning and one abounding in travail, for it doesn't take a geologist to tell that its father was either a volcano or an earthquake and its mama an old crater—when, as I say, this interesting event took place, the Supreme Designer failed, under two counts and two counts only, to complete His masterpiece. He didn't coin a word or a set of words competent to sum up its beauties. And by a similar defect of the omnipotent judgment, He didn't put any fish in it to begin with.

And so it was that because of this latter oversight, Maligne Lake went along fishless for quite a few million years, the exact number of millions for the moment escaping me. In fact it went along that way until quite a spell after what is now the main line of the Canadian National had nosed through a convenient gap just north of it and the Canadian Government had incorporated it into Jasper National Park, the largest national park in the world, and to my way of thinking, in some regards the most picturesque and the most fascinating national park in North America. Indeed it remained fishless until some fifteen years ago when, having first made sure that its waters held plenty of fish food, the management experimentally introduced into Maligne Lake a supply of fingerling brook trout, selected, by a process of elimination, from streams in western Pennsylvania. The affair started off as an experiment; it turned into a piscatorial miracle, so rapidly did that transplanted Eastern small fry grow, so amazingly did it multiply, so game, so strong, so heavy and so valiant did its get become under the influences of a benign combination of rushing rapids, mile-high climate, golden shallows, glacier-fed source streams, and the ice-water temperature of tremendous greenish-blue depths so richly aerated that fat round bubbles rise constantly to the surface like fairy balloons.

I assisted, semiformally, as it were, in the dedication of Maligne Lake to the gentle art of casting. After five days on a railroad train I arrived there at the start of the last week in June, which would be rather late for good brook-trout fishing anywhere back East, and much too late for it farther south, but because of the altitude and the weather conditions born of that altitude, was really just the beginning of the season in the Canadian Highlands. In parentheses, as it were, I might insert here that this is where Maligne Lake as a fishing ground has a decided advantage over most other fishing grounds in the Temperate Zone. Elsewhere you must go into camp early and fight the black fly, a champion who never yet lost the decision on points, and take the risk of running into a belated cold snap; or go later and endure the attentions of Br'er Skeeter and Sis' Deerfly, whereas at Maligne the middle of the midsummer vacation marks the peak of the best fishing, so that during a ten-weeks' period a fellow may be sure of getting the very cream of the sport in a magic land where the insect pests are few and feeble, where the air is like spicy mulled wine when the sun shines, and like breaths of chilled perfume when the sun goes down; where the days are never too warm and very

rarely are too cool for comfort, and the fragrant darkness calls
always for that extra blanket. One hot night in Jasper Park
would start a lot of trouble for the authorities. The folks who
live up there just naturally wouldn't stand for it.

I never knew there were such trout—trout so vivid in their
coloring, so uniformly heavy for their age, so savage at striking
and so gallant in the battle which follows the strike. For all
their fecundity and their incalculable number—I'm sure this
is one place which will never, as the saying goes, be "fished out"
—there are times when it takes plenty of coaxing to induce
them to rise, and that makes for real angling skill. Again
there are times when the stilled eddies seem literally to be
boiling with gamboling big ones. On such a day your true
fisherman turns his back on these swarming hordes and goes
after the shyer, warier warriors that live in the rapids of
Maligne River, a loud-talking quarrelsome stream which runs
into the lake at one side and runs out at the foot to go tumbling
downhill at the rate of over 1,000 feet in an eleven-mile stretch,
and then after widening out again to form Medicine Lake,
dives into a mountain and wanders through a subterranean
passage for nobody knows how far before it emerges out in
the valley—an idiosyncrasy not uncommon among such brawling rivers in the Rockies.

The unexpectedly swift transformation of Maligne Lake
from barren waters to fruitful waters rather took those in
charge of the development by surprise. The result was that for
the first open season the management had to impress ranch
hands and big-game trackers for guide service. To see a cowboy, in high-heeled boots and floppy hat, trying to look at
home in a tippy canoe was a spectacle worth traveling a thousand miles to see. And to study that veteran professional
hunter and stalker, the illustrious Jack Brewster, vainly en-

deavoring to figure out in his own mind how a presumably
rational creature could be satisfied to whip the same spot for
half an hour just to snag onto a fish weighing merely a couple
of pounds or so, when if the poor idiot only would wait until
fall he could go out with a rifle and fatally undermine a bull
moose as big as a plantation mule—well, that's a precious
memory too!

Nowadays there is available a troupe of expert fishing guides
and paddlers for duty on Maligne. Also there was continued
an airplane-transport schedule inaugurated after I was there—
fifteen minutes from the dainty little lake fronting Jasper Park
Lodge over the peaks to Maligne Lake. But as for me, if
ever I return, I shall follow the slower route—by automobile to Medicine Lake, thence the length of Medicine by
launch, thence by horseback along the climbing winding
trail beside the river and through a noble forest that never
knew blight nor fire nor the woodman's ax up, up to the
foot of Maligne, with its comfortable log chalets, and its pretty
hostess and its staff of pleasant girl helpers and its attendant
tent colony. Because, going that way you see the wild life that
fairly teems in Jasper—among other natives we meet a mother
grizzly and her two shambling yearling cubs. You see moose
and mule deer in the mountain meadows, and possibly you see
brown and black bears browsing on the berries in the thickets
and you see the skipping bighorn sheep—not individually but
in big herds—on the flanks of one mountain, and on the bare
upper nape of its neighbor mayhap you count five, ten, possibly
twenty moving white dots and know that each dot is a wild
goat. Or if your fancy inclines more to flora than to fauna
you may see such a prodigal wealth of wild buds and wild blos-
soms as you never dreamed of. And if you are a scenery lover
—well, somehow that seems to bring me back to the subject of

the scenery and reminds one of the one flaw, the one drawback, in this delectable chalice of beauty and sport.

The trouble is this: If you are both a scenery-drunkard and a lover of trout-fishing, as I claim to be, the surrounding vistas are so gorgeous that your temptation is to quit fishing and go to looking, while on the other hand the fishing is so good you feel you must quit looking and go back to fishing; and naturally that unsettles a fellow's mental poise and brings on nervous exhaustion and the galloping jitters. You get to be like the feeble-minded milkman who, stool and pail in hand, stood irresolute between his prize pair of cows and murmured: "I could be happy with either, were udder dear charmer away."

When I speak of the scenery I think not so much of the lower end of Maligne, although the view there is sufficiently magnificent for the uplifting of anyone's awed soul, nor of the stretches of the river where, past each turn, is a dazzling new backdrop of great boulders and roaring flaunting cataracts, with the moss-grown banks and the splendid tall evergreens to frame the picture in, and always, for a further background, the encompassing peaks marching in mighty processionals. What especially I think of is the crowning sublimity of the upper end of Maligne Lake, within the Narrows, so-called.

Your launch or your skiff rounds the outthrust shoulder of a tremendous inner gateway and at once the illusion is that you are completely hemmed in, that you have been imprisoned forevermore within a vast yet intimate basin from which there is no escape. You are at a height of approximately one mile above sea level—floating upon waters which under the alternate bandings of shadow and light are here the greenest green that ever was and there a bluer blue than any artist yet found in his paint tubes and yonder, under the verge of the encircling walls, appear to be purplish-black. And when your oar splashes up this water the spray falls back as sparkling jewels, as emeralds and glowing rubies and brilliant diamonds and amethysts and star sapphires, and opals and great globular iridescent pearls.

Being dwarfed by what surrounds it, the lake seems here to be but a pool. Its foreshortened edges end at bright gravel banks, and behind them in turn are briefened areas of gently rising ground, polka-dotted with billions of giddy, gaudy wild flowers and grooved by splashing cataracts and finished off with close ranks of pine and spruce. Immediately then, as the slopes steepen, the vegetation tails off to scrub, and in rifts and in shallow gorges against the buttresses of the greater heights are snowbanks. Even in midsummer you see them up above and beyond you, and often saffron lilies are growing and blooming through the white drifts. Higher still are the gleaming saddlecloths of the glaciers which at their upper levels tail away into the everlasting ice fields and at their bases melt into thin filmy falls that are like living bridal veils foaming down all about you. And then, for a final stroke, the sheared and shorn pinnacles of the mountains climb straight up—not sloped, not indented, nor benched, but cut smack off as smooth and as true as masonry. They rise up and up, and, rising, shade from gray to brown and from brown to umber and from umber to tan, and mount and mount in breath-taking leaps until their sun-burnished crests, which seem to be threatening to fold in and crush you, are yet another mile aloft.

Beforehand you cannot imagine what this vision is like. While you're there your numbed senses scarce can comprehend it, and afterward your memory reels at the effort to rebuild the terrifying, electrifying image of it.

So I'll just say this—if you can conceive a sizable segment of Lake Tahoe as being buried at the bottom of the Grand

Canyon—if you can do that without straining yourself, why then maybe you'll begin to have a faint and shadowy and sketchy notion of the rough idea."

The hardest trips into the wilds never seemed to tire him. He grew merry, not to say roguish, over all the incumbent hardships. He was not only willing, he was delighted to find himself cold, wet, bone-tired, hungry and lost, and yet anyone who ever saw him going about the daily necessary chores of everyday living must have realized that nothing was easy for him, such heavy weather did he make of any task that did not involve some sort of woodcraft. To make things harder for himself, he was a perfectionist; he would have everything just so, or beat his brains out trying.

Catch a train with him . . . oh, my! To be sure, his tickets would be ready in one hand, his loose change in the other, his bags marked and counted, and he himself in such good time that he was often able to read a light novel between the hour of his arrival at the station and that of his departure from it. And the effort required to arrange all thus was so great that not only would he be exhausted but everybody else around him, including hardened old conductors and strong young porters.

I remember once when we two set off on a holiday together. We were going to New Orleans and then to Houston for a stop with the Hoggs and finally through Eagle Pass, Texas, and across the border to be the guest of Hal Mangum (and a salute to you, Don Mango!) at Rancho La Barbia, which is just simply the most wonderful place left on this earth. (Seventeen guns went forth one morning from La Barbia; seventeen wild turkeys, big, fat ones, hung in the storehouse that evening. Why, I've got some South Carolina pals who think seventeen wild turkeys is a record for a decade, not a morning!)

Well, naturally, when starting off on this jaunt we were anticipating no pain, indeed the contrary. Now as I knew the man well I wasn't idiot enough to arrive at the station at the last moment. And find him all worked up into a snit? Not me! I was there some forty minutes before the train was due to depart, which seems a reasonably ample margin of time. After all, we weren't going to have to fight our way onto a Chinese refugee train. We weren't *escaping* anywhere. We had a drawing room, which we had quite openly and honestly bought and paid for, on a streamline train, filled only to about half its capacity, a train, moreover, which had never indulged in any little eccentricities like changing the time of its departure without due and official notice to all interested parties, including passengers.

He'd beat me there, of course, by a good fifteen minutes, and although not getting really anxious yet about my tardiness was prepared to be so almost instantly. I could tell that by the stern eye he bent upon me and the quick follow-up glance at the station clock.

"Humph," he said, "so you got here! Where's your baggage?"

"Your porter has it."

"Oh! But naturally you didn't count it? I never knew a woman yet ever had the slightest notion how much luggage she was toting with her."

"I have three pieces. A large bag. Tan. A hatbox. Also tan. And a small dressing case. Black."

"Oh!"

"I think I'll go buy the papers and some magazines—I'll be right back."

"You'll do no such thing . . . start wandering around by yourself, get lost, miss us this train! You stay right here beside me where I can keep an eye on you."

"Yes, sir, boss!" I said, slipping my arm through his.

"Now don't do that! Great heavens . . . how can I look after things if you plant yourself directly on top of me? . . . Haven't you any sense at all? I don't want you underfoot, woman!"

"Do you know what?" I said. "I don't think I'm going to Mexico after all. I think I've had about all of this trip I can take. . . . So good-by, darling. . . . Certainly did have a fine time, didn't we?"

"Listen, Buff," he said: "if you are going to start out cross there isn't a bit of use our going at all. What in the world is the matter with you anyhow? Sometimes I think you're sort of simple in the head. . . . Now would you mind telling me just *what* has made you angry?"

I just looked at him. He had the grace to blush. For the rest of the trip his manners were Chesterfieldian and his benevolence equaled that of a buck-angel.

But catching trains with him . . . well now, that was something else again!

And he was like that about so many things, so plagued and bothered. Why, a ride in a taxi with him would leave the driver a nervous wreck and a companion hanging onto his nerves like grim death, if at all.

After we moved to California I drove him a lot. He would sit well forward in the back seat, the better to keep an eye on things, and hold tight to the sides, and direct. Incidentally he had only once ever so much as attempted to drive any sort or description of mechanically propelled vehicle. That time he knocked down a new cement wall.

"Why are you stopping? . . . You know I'm in a hurry."

"Red light."

"What's that got to do with it?"

"Nothing, really. Only if I drive on past the light when it is red, that fine upstanding young policeman just across the street will see me do it—and then he will stop us, with machine-gun fire if necessary, or, if I pull over when he says to, he *might* give us a break, and in that case it will only cost you five bucks."

"Oh! More fool rules and regulations out here."

The light changes; I go on.

"Thought you couldn't go through that light."

"Only when it's red. It is green. When it's green we go."

"Oh!"

Oh! Oh! Oh! *Oh!*

Keep him waiting for his dinner and he was a man demoralized, not because he was so greedy but because he was so nervous.

This had been true of him in his youth; he was ever the prey of nervous irritation, but then it had come only in momentary flashes, like a flicker of far-off, quick, harmless heat lightning. After he came back from the war in '14 it was truer than ever, and all but uncontrollably so.

Laura did not understand. She knew that he had been under a great strain, that he was tired and greatly in need of a rest, and of having only gentle, quiet people around him, but she could not help being puzzled and hurt, when rest and the loving welcome, and even the stimulation of a great personal success, seemed to make no difference and he remained, month after month, year after year, so cross . . . so strange! Yes, that is the word. He was a stranger. He clung to his home, but it was as one who is afraid that he will be lost forever if he quits it, not as one who is happy to be there. As for those who shared it with him, those whom he loved so tenderly and so deeply, why, it seemed that though he was more than willing to take care of them, and continue to live with them, he was simply not very interested in them any more. That was it. He was not interested.

It was while this book was being written, and no sooner, that we found out quite by accident what had happened to him. One day my daughter, who is eighteen now, and my mother and I were talking about Dad, and Pat absolutely flabbergasted us by remarking casually, "Well, I guess he never did really get over his attack of shell shock."

We were at lunch, and my mother put down her fork and turned deadly white.

"What do you mean?" she demanded. "Irvin never had shell shock."

"He told me that he did," Pat said, and then seeing how greatly her grandmother was affected, "But surely you knew?" she asked.

"No," said Laura sadly, "no—I never knew. How did you know?"

"Why, he told me," Pat said, "years ago, when I was a very little girl. We were down at East Hampton and I had been asking him about the war. He said that he had had shell shock, not badly, but enough so that a thunderstorm, or any loud noise affected him very strangely."

"How?" demanded Laura.

"Why, the noise made him go to sleep—right off, as though he had taken a drug so that it was almost impossible to wake him. And he said that some English general or other had told him that this was a rare and usually very serious form of shock."

And until he wrote this in his autobiography when he was an old man he never told any soul, not even his doctors, except a six-year-old child.

No wonder he seemed a stranger. He *was* a stranger, and to himself most of all.

There will be many a good man coming home to his family after this war who will suffer the same disorientation and for the same reason, and try as valiantly to conceal his troubled sense of loneliness and apartness from his folks, for fear of worrying them! For fear of worrying them! Or perhaps from shame of what he thinks is a weakness. It is so pitiful. And it is so tragic. And so grand. And so stupid!

I wonder if those lecture tours, undertaken almost immediately after his return, were a good thing for him, as well as for his career? Certainly he was tremendously stimulated by his contact with an audience, although scared almost to death at first, a fact which those who have heard him, and felt the impart of his ease and authority when on a platform, find hard to believe. I will never forget the little horrified cry that my mother gave from her box at Carnegie Hall the first night that he spoke, when a woman sitting very close to the platform suddenly keeled over in a faint. Laura was sorry for the woman; she was also in mortal terror that this interruption might throw Dad off so badly that he would be unable to collect his thoughts or his audience, knowing as she did just how fragile and uncertain was his poise. When he filled a glass of water from the pitcher provided for him on the rostrum, and signaled an usher to come up to him and get it, and then waited, seemingly quite at his ease, without speaking until he saw that the woman had regained consciousness and was all right, and then went ahead exactly as though nothing had happened to put him off his stride (only now of course his hearers were deeply in sympathy with him, perhaps not knowing quite why, but liking him tremendously), I heard Laura let the air out of her lungs with a gasp, like someone who has been a long time under water. She had come near fainting herself, she says.

From then on audiences became of increasing importance to

him. They brought him to life, or to it gave an accentuation and clarity that was lost for him without their aid. They excited him, and nothing else did. Whether a man suffering from incipient or half-cured shell shock ought to be thus excited I don't know, but I doubt it.

He never complained about the strain of these trips, and indeed we did not realize that he was under one until he suddenly collapsed one night and came about as near cashing in as a man can without making a complete job of it.

Even then we thought that this was the result of the fantastic, the almost incredible treatment he had devised to cope with an attack of flu—that deadly wartime flu which was still abroad in the land. Refusing to cancel a single engagement, or even to go to bed in between them, he doggedly continued his tour, living for several days on handfuls of aspirin, to which it was afterward discovered that he was allergic, and priming himself for travel and talks by nips from a flask of bootleg whisky. He found that he was not relishing his food very much, so one night, to perk up his appetite, he supped off a large helping of pickled pigs' feet. He said afterward that he had figured that if pickled pigs' feet didn't cure him of what ailed him he'd call in a doctor. Strangely enough, they were no cure-all, so the next day, again putting off the dread moment of asking for medical advice, he had some more aspirin, some more whisky and two dozen of those outsize New England oysters.

The Boston physician who finally examined him, and gave him at the most but a few hours to live, said that his liver had turned into as hard a rock as any you could find on a Massachusetts hillside. He said that the Pilgrim Fathers could have landed on him. A blood vessel had burst, and some six weeks later, when he was brought home on a stretcher, he was still whiter than the pillow under his head, dead-white, gray-white, sick-white—that ruddy, "high-complected" man—and thus his family began to catch onto the fact that perhaps Pa had been peaked for quite a spell. We were reminded of that old story Dad used to tell. Once there was a man whose wife was forever ailing. For years she went from doctor to doctor, from cure to cure, finally she died, and when her husband saw her lying in her coffin he wagged his head sadly and said, "Well, after all, maybe Mama was sick."

When Irvin came home from those long, tiring trips, he never told us of the hard parts, only of the funny ones. Of the drunk, for instance, in some town out West, who had wandered into the theater under the misapprehension that therein was some rather livelier spectacle than a lone man giving a speech on the war. He was disappointed when the truth dawned on him and he desired to leave, but he was much too drunk to negotiate the steep incline that was the only available exit from his balcony seat. Again and again he clattered up the aisle, again and again he fell down it. And not quietly, either, but causing only slightly less noise than if he had been provided with firearms. This, of course, was not making things any too easy for Irvin, who began to feel that he would prefer playing in opposition to a three-alarm fire.

When this unfortunate gentleman fell for the last time down the aisle, he fetched up half over the balcony railings. An inch more and he'd have been a goner and what's worse have landed on some perfectly innocent people seated below him. I'll bet they wouldn't have been the right people to fall on from a great height either. He was saved, and removed, to his audible relief, from the railing and the theater by a pair of quick-moving ushers, and Dad and the audience settled down to the lecture again. Ten minutes or so of blessed peace went by, and then back came our friend. Now he was equipped with a new ticket, to an orchestra seat this time, and judging from the smile of expectancy illuminating his countenance, was under the impression that he was in an entirely different theater from the one from which he had recently had such a hard time escaping. He clattered happily down the center aisle, then his eyes focused on the stage, the rostrum, the lone lecturer, and he froze in his tracks. "My God!" he said in outraged voice. "This damn foolishness is going on all over town!"

And there were the Demon Introducers. Every lecturer has tales to tell of this strange breed, but certainly Dad drew some beauts. For instance there was the Demon Introducer who presented him to his audience as "Irving Batcheller," and then dimly feeling that this was perhaps not quite right somehow tried to fix it up by adding, "Whom you all know and love as the author of *Fables in Slang*."

But for really torturing a lecturer the device thought up by another of his D. I.'s has never been bettered, I think. This one rose, a smiling villain, and started his fell work most graciously by saying that it had been his pleasure and privilege to hear Mr. Cobb a week before, and on that memorable occasion he had told them some wonderful things. For instance . . . And then, for forty-five minutes by the clock, he gave Dad's lecture. All of it. For instance, indeed! Dad said that he sat there on that platform sweating an ice-cold sweat and all but audibly praying that he could think up a new talk before this man finished giving the current one, and, if this were not possible, that at least one of his own stories—just one of his heart's darlings—might be spared to him. . . . But no. The D. I. didn't miss one. He was evidently a person with a remarkable memory, the gift of close observation and, of course, a delight in the sound of his own voice.

I have entitled this chapter "A Long Ride Down Easy Street." We had that all right. Whether Easy Street is such a

hot place is open to question. I like it fine, but then I had the
ride given to me. And what's more—lots more—a sojourn in
this hard-won-to but very dull district was not my big reward
for being a good girl. They say that one can lead a donkey for
miles and miles by holding a carrot just in front of its nose . . .
seems a slim reward for a long trek, especially if it isn't a very
juicy carrot, or what's even worse if the authorities decide to
withdraw the carrot entirely, and save it for another day—or
another donkey.

In other words I don't think that most Americans after they
get rich have very much fun any more. Or perhaps in every
land, and every kind of civilization, it has always been the
struggle up the hill that's great, and not the view from the top.
A wise and witty friend of mine (as a slight hint to her iden-
tity I will tell you that she is blonde, and lovely to look upon,
and gets herself elected to Congress from time to time) told
me that she could never get over the extraordinary dullness of
life with the very, very rich in Newport, until she figured out
that the inhabitants, believing that they had reached the pinnacle, were all slightly afflicted with a touch of the vertigo
natural to rarefied heights, and so all crawled around on their
hands and knees for fear of falling off.

Well, naturally my folks never had enough money to pay
even the initiation fee to Newport, but from any other standards
they were darned well fixed—but not having much fun. Again
I am talking about Laura and Irvin, especially Irvin. Laura
loved parties, her kind of parties—that is, informal, merry
ones, never the large, pompous kind—and pretty clothes, and
trips to Europe, which he detested.

We lured him over once or twice, and after he had taken
one walk through a strange town, and found out where the
American Express was located, he behaved exactly like that
elephant in Kipling's story who got fractious and bored and

not only refused to work himself but would not let anyone else work either.

He came to stay with me in Florence for several weeks just before Pat was born, when Frank and I were living in a very comfortable villino out near Fiesole. We had a lot of amusing friends, and what we thought a very pleasant life, but he was so bored with life in a foreign town that I think he went home convinced that we were two of the most unfortunate young people alive.

Before Pat decided to put in an appearance, which was just six weeks after she was expected, he grew so miserable that I honestly thought if the baby didn't get on with being born, I was either going to lose my mind—or my poor Pa. Bob Davis was there at the same time, and behaving in the same way. They haunted the American Express, badgering the clerks for mail which was not there, and could not be there, as they perfectly well knew, because of the necessity of transporting it from America in ships which, although running regularly, did not run every hour on the hour. This they refused to admit, conducting themselves as though convinced that they were victims of a deliberate conspiracy set in motion by the authorities for the explicit purpose of defrauding them of their correspondence.

They would not go sight-seeing, or on expeditions into the country, no—they paced around and groused and yawned and grumbled, and went to the American Express. I never saw two grown men more in need of having their ears boxed.

This conduct was the more peculiarly exasperating because they were men who should have enjoyed the city of Florence enormously. They were historically minded, they had keen eyes and sensitive perceptions to bring to the town where even the stones of the streets are eloquent. But no! They conducted themselves as much like a pair of illiterate cattle drovers on a world tour as was possible, continually repeating with a relish no one else savored that deplorable old story of the two American tourists who arrive one morning at the Louvre where one of them says to the other, "You take the inside, I'll take the outside and I'll meet you here in ten minutes."

Then they would sit around my house and talk about things to eat, but never by any chance things to eat that were obtainable in Tuscany. They were eloquent indeed on the subject of chicken cooked in fresh coconuts, as they do it in Hawaii, or the manifold virtues of turnip greens Missouri-style. They merely ate my cook's homemade green noodles and *orsi bucci* in sullen silence.

Also they were deeply impressed with Mussolini—as was practically all of America in those first days when Fascism was honeymooning with the world. Well, it was ever a shotgun wedding. We who had the privilege of living under the regime for over two years were beginning to suspect this, were actually not overwhelmed with gratitude that "there were no beggars on the streets, and the trains always ran on time." Lordy! how tired we got of that phrase!

There were no beggars because they were dead, or better dead, and those punctual trains were running to some mighty unpleasant places, but when we suggested as much to Bob and Dad, they roared us down as young malcontents, ignorant and subversive children who did not know what we were talking about. And indeed we didn't. No one living in Italy at that time knew anything. The government saw to that. But we had begun to sense the wrongness of things, the inherent evil lurking along in the wake of the big parade. There was a smell. . . .

I wanted Dad to find out what was causing it. I wanted him and Bob to take their foot in their hand and go for to see and go for to find out, and then go home and tell the world. There never lived two more courageous men, or two cannier, and if it had ever dawned on either one of them that those attractive young men in the pretty uniforms who made such a fuss over them at the Chigi Palace were merely a bunch of well-dressed mobsters, or that the whole of Italy was as much delivered into the hands of a gang as ever Chicago was to Capone's boys, why, they would have cut loose with a journalistic blast to rattle the very bones in the Catacombs. But they were not bothering themselves about the vague apprehensions of a chit of a girl, and the men who might have enlightened them were too busy, being actively engaged at that time with making little ones out of big ones in the prisons of the Dodecanese Islands, or in swallowing a quart or two of castor oil and in dying from the results.

In some ways I think that this blindness was a deliberate limitation of vision, not a congenital myopia, and the reason was that the majority of the people of the United States were for Mussolini, and what the United States liked Irvin Cobb liked. He was, both deliberately and instinctively, Mr. Average Citizen. Perhaps that is why so many Americans were so very fond of him. He was themselves, grown famous. Even his eccentricities were such American ones that most people felt tender toward them and respected them just as they do their own.

So when I insisted that he look at Italian Primitives, and he all but literally shut his eyes, muttering that he would give every old master that ever lived for one Remington or a couple of Charley Russells, I, knowing that he had started life with the ambition of being an artist and that if he would only look, just one good look, he would see, and seeing enjoy, and enjoying be enriched, was intensely annoyed with him. I thought he was being exceedingly stupid. Now I think that it was I who was the stupid one. The man was unconsciously protecting his prejudices because he needed them in his business.

A couple of years later Dad and his beloved friend, the unique, the fascinating, the incalculable Will Hogg of Houston, Texas, went off on a jaunt together through South America. They turned up after many months in the south of France where Laura and I were on hand to welcome them looking a little weather-beaten but still speaking, which was proof of their deep and abiding affection, for if ever a cat and a dog went on a trip together it was those two. Will wanted to stay up all night and sleep all day; Dad wanted to rise with the merry, merry, merry dawn and turn in soon as it was dark. Cat and dog, or better, cat and rooster. They must have been a funny pair!

Of course Dad, when he was awake, was heavenly to have along on any little jaunt or expedition because he could always be counted on for at least one spontaneous crack that would set you rocking with laughter. So many of those wonderful moments are lost. I cannot remember what it was that set us screaming with mirth to the alarm and mystification of the natives; I can only remember the instant of comprehension, the lovely clean feeling of release, the blessed bodily seizure that comes with an honest belly laugh. And Dad, never laughing himself, waiting, and wearing mischief like a halo, until the first convulsion was almost spent, and then doubling you up again, as he did the day we were wandering about the tortured, ancient, crazy quilt of a town called Eze where the streets remind one of the Gadarene swine, for they seem possessed of devils; they run down from a high place and they cast themselves into the sea. There we were approached by a very tattered, very smelly gentleman who, with considerable hauteur, made it known to us that it was now about to be our privilege to bestow alms upon him. I know that this is a most awkward and roundabout way to say that an old man begged from us, but then you see his manner was such that you could not think about the transaction in those crude terms and I find it impossible to be less windy and yet describe the subtle distinction of his manners, or the delicate nuances of his address. Dad, considerably impressed, slipped this hidalgo some twenty francs. He looked at the money. He looked at Dad. He threw the inadequate tribute to the earth and cursed us all impartially, then picked up the money, turned his back upon us and stalked off in affronted silence.

"My God!" said Dad. "Look at him. Even the seat of his pants is making faces at me!" And it was!

If that old man is still alive I'll bet he is still wondering why those mad Americans all suddenly began to gasp with laughter at being cursed.

Laura says that Dad and Bob were even more fractious on the boat going home than they had been in Florence, so bored and cross and restless that finally she could not bear them another moment and bullied them into letting her teach them Russian Bank. This saved their respective reasons, and hers, but it almost broke up a lifelong friendship, they took it that seriously and cheated each other so enthusiastically. They were hardly speaking by the time the boat got in, because the day before Irvin had made a brilliant and masterful move, and was sitting back to crow and pleasure himself and collect when Bob cried out, "Hold on there—you can't do that. It's against the rules."

"Why, you so-and-so of a so-and-so," cried Dad, "didn't you just do exactly that to me, not a minute ago?"

"Yes, but . . ."

"No buts about it . . . you owe me three dollars."

Bob was stumped for a second, but only for a second. He rallied fast, and said, "I do not! . . . You see that move can be used only once in each game."

It was during that visit that we gave a musicale, which is

certainly not a form of entertainment that I would have subjected him to by choice, his or mine. It just happened that some very important musical people, who could be of immense help to Frank, who was after all living in Italy for the purpose of studying singing, happened to arrive from Rome and the party was given for them and Dad attended because of having nothing better to do.

We managed a very successful lunch, they were most pleasant people and the food and wine were as good as planned, a rare occurrence anywhere, all but unique in ours, where the cook was wont to lose the remnants of her aged wits as soon as company came, and afterward Frank was going to sing, and, so that all the talent on display be not strictly home-grown, we asked a composer friend of ours to play his newest symphony. Frank sang first, then our friend took possession of the piano, and as I knew that the first part of his composition was very loud indeed, and I would not be noticed, I slipped out to give some order concerning drinks and stuff to the servants. As I emerged from the pantry I found that Dad had followed and was standing in the little back hall waiting for me. Feeling very pleased with everything, I was in that blissful state that descends upon a nervous young hostess when she knows that her party is not only going well but going home pretty soon. But the glow went out of me when I saw Dad's poor sad face. He didn't say a word, he just put his arms around me, and gave me a hug, and then very gently and sadly, "Oh, my poor baby! I know you have to put up with a lot of music. Your old Dad certainly is sorry for you!"

Moie and Dad had enjoyed the building of our house out in the hills behind Ossining in Westchester (Step 4. Real country), but I think more the planning than the building, and more the building than the subsequent living there. They were both strangely restless. As for me, at first I detested the place because I was lonely there, and growing up to the age when I craved the company of vast crowds of young people ... not caring much what kind of young people, just wanting great lots of them around all the time, emitting continuous loud cries and forever going somewhere, in a Stutz Bearcat roadster.

They had chosen our part of Westchester because a great many of their friends were settled there, most amusing people—actors and writers and such folk—George Creel, Blanche Bates, Margaret Illington and her husband Major Eddy Bowes, Margaret Mayo and her husband Edgar Selwyn, Mr. and Mrs. James Forbes, Holbrook and Ruth Blinn, charming all ... but childless. Times have certainly changed. Nowadays it's the artists who set up the big old-fashioned families, just as nowadays a really pretty and chic girl is just as apt to be the author of the latest best-seller as a chorus girl. Dad used to say that he was able to spot a lady writer at twenty paces, because the grime on the neck was clearly visible at that distance, and that a lady with a really dirty face was either working in a coal mine or on a new novel. If she wore four or five pounds of assorted "art" jewelry she was not working in a coal mine.

At last I got a big break because Adelaide and Rupert Hughes moved to within twelve miles of us, and I had their children, the fabulous Rush and Avis, to play with. Then Laura grew friendly with Colonel and Mrs. Ben McAlpin and they had had the perspicacity to provide themselves with three exceedingly good-looking sons—good-looking and going to Princeton yet! Life—it's wonderful!

But poor Irvin was soon fairly awash in a wave of large, noisy youths, who quite naturally thought him a senile old character to whom it was necessary to be courteous, they having been taught nice manners by their families, but who should not be encouraged to enter into the conversation or otherwise spoil the fun. I quite agreed with them because I thought that he probably couldn't be much less than ninety years old, and though a darling, a fragile one with weird antediluvian notions concerning the necessity of returning home at least twice a week before three in the morning. One had to indulge him, at least one had to pretend to indulge him, to the extent of taking off one's shoes when going upstairs, and making the boys keep the drinks parked in the car. Of course anybody over thirty was so old to me that I couldn't for the life of me see how they supported their dreary ancient days, and Dad must have been past forty—the poor old wretch!

My mother opened the house to my friends, doing for me what her mama and papa had done for her, and the place was always full of them. I can't ever remember sitting down to the table alone, nor hardly remember there ever being many older people among those present; occasionally a few might be sprinkled around, in a tiresome sort of way, but they were kept down, and humble. Great Lord, how bored they must have been! What am I saying? Must have been, indeed! Were! Jimmy Forbes, who later became a great friend of mine, told me that it was just dreadful! He said that he and Jean would drive home from our house, most low in their minds, and plotting how to save poor dear Laura and Irvin from their fate.

"What was the worst part?" I asked him.

"The boys, of course. At least the girls were nice to look at."

"But the girls make the most noise."

"I know. It's awful! But the boys—" and then very explosively—"boys are so condescending! And . . . and, dammit, they have so much hair!"

Laura tells me that once Dad was driven to appealing to

her. "Look here," he expostulated. "I have a big house, and six servants to run it, and sixty acres—and I haven't any place to sit down or any place to go take a walk."

Dad, being no fool, did have his workroom detached from the main house, and it seems to me that I only remember him in those days as a dim figure who occasionally emerged onto his little porch to yell something at a gardener, and who was usually good for a touch. Also I would encounter him now and then coming from long walks in the woods back up on the ridge, a lovely spot alive with birds including the ruffled grouse, walks on which he was escorted by a sad-eyed setter that someone had given him, an enormous animal suffering from the delusion that he was a lap dog. Of him Dad remarked that he was the very spit of a certain financier and patron of the arts, greatly in the news of the day for, "one kind word and he climbs in your lap and wants to join your club."

On the other hand the real lap dog, Ku Ti, a Pekinese, and a most charming person, thought that he was a setter. A setter or a lion, depending upon the day and his mood. It was most touching to watch Ku Ti try to imitate the expert on their daily walks, pointing when he pointed, freezing when he froze, trying his best but never able to uncurl his poor tail, nor get his ridiculous nose out into the scent. I am quite sure that he never smelled anything—how could he with his equipment? —but one never laughed at him. It didn't hurt his feelings, or if it did he never sulked; he merely bit you neatly and quickly and then forgave you at once.

Later on, when I grew up somewhat, I experienced a rather wonderful sense of the kaleidoscoping of time, as though the years between us had been folded up in such a small compass that they could be packed away and forgotten. In other words I was still his daughter, but a daughter as old as he, who could thus be his friend as well. Then we used to talk about those days, and laugh a little but with tenderness, and I told him that I didn't see how he stood it.

"I don't either," he said. "I guess I was reasonably fond of you."

"But even so . . ."

"But even so it was pretty bad."

"Why did you put up with it?"

"Oh, I don't know. . . . Kids . . . You just do, that's all. . . . And then, thank God! I was working hard."

"Moie was working hard, too," I said, "running the place and the parties. . . ."

"Well, of course she was. . . . The woman had to hang on to her sanity somehow, didn't she?"

He was working very hard indeed, of course, for we were all gleefully spending all the money we could lay our hands on, he just as bad as Laura and I, for he developed some very pretty notions of his own in regard to bluestone roads, and terraces down to the lake. Of that road, which ran a little over a quarter of a mile from the gate to the garage, he wrote in a book called *The Abandoned Farmers*.

When we got in the estimates on the job we decided that the contractor must have figured on building our road of chalcedony or onyx or moss agate or some other of the semi-precious stones. It didn't seem possible that he meant to use any native material—at that price. It turned out, though, that his bid was fairly moderate—as processed bluestone roads go in this climate; and ours has cost us only about eight times as much as I had previously supposed a replica of the Appian Way would cost. However, it has been pronounced a very good road by critics who should know; not a fancy road, but a fair average one.

Also, he wrote a very funny piece in the same book about the stout resistance he put up against antique furniture, and how his resolution to keep it out of his house (yes, if he were to be the last man alive using a Grand Rapids "suite") was undermined by the artfulness of the ladies in his immediate family. And there isn't a word of truth in it! He was just as infatuated a creature as Laura, though sometimes his attempts at interior decorating were odd, not to say outrageous. Witness the many stalwart efforts he made to hang bits of his Indian collection in the Italian dining room. There's certainly nothing like a chief's war bonnet to give a refectory table a certain *je-ne-sais-quoi*. . . .

This is his account . . . and 'taint so! At least 'taint all so.

"You must remember," I was told, "that for the six or eight years before we decided to move out here to the country we lived in a flat."

"What of it?" I retorted instantly. "What of it?" I repeated, for when in the heat of controversy I think up an apt bit of repartee like that I am apt to utter it a second time for the sake of emphasis. Pausing only to see if my stroke of instantaneous retort had struck in, I continued:

"That last flat we had swallowed up furniture as a rat hole swallows sand. First and last we must have poured enough stuff into that flat to furnish the state of Rhode Island." . . .

"Don't be absurd," I was admonished. "Just compare the size of the largest bedroom in that last flat we had . . . with the size of the smallest bedroom we expect to have in the new place. Why, you could put the biggest bedroom we had there into the smallest bedroom we are going to have here and lose it! And then think of the halls we must furnish and the living room and the breakfast porch and everything. Did we have a breakfast porch in the flat? We did not! Did we have a living room forty feet one way and twenty-eight the other? We did not! Did we have a dining room in that flat that was big enough to swing a cat in?"

"We didn't have any cat."

"All the same, we——"

"I doubt whether any of the neighbors would have loaned us a cat just for that purpose." I felt I had the upper hand and I meant to keep it. "Besides, you know I don't like cats. What is the use of importing foreign matters such as cats—and purely problematical cats at that—into a discussion about something else? What relation does a cat bear to furniture, I ask you? Still, speaking of cats, I'm reminded——"

"Never mind trying to be funny! And never mind trying to steer the conversation off the right track either . . . let's see—where was I? Oh, yes: did we have a hall in that flat worthy to be dignified by the name of a hall? We did not! We had a passageway—that's what it was—a passageway. Now there is a difference between furnishing a mere passageway and a regular hall, as you are about to discover before you are many months older." . . .

But conceded that the reader is but a humble husbandman—meaning by that a man who is married—he doubtless has already figured out the result of this debate. . . . In the end I surrendered. . . . From that hour dated the beginning of my wider and fuller education into the system commonly in vogue . . . for the furnishing of homes."

While the "big house" was being built we lived in the top of a remodeled barn. This had been planned only as a temporary expedient, but the war came along and stopped the work, so that we were barnyarders for several years.

It was a long time later before I understood what the building of a home could mean. In those days I used to watch my parents perched on a rock pile in the pouring rain, quite oblivious of wet, weariness or weather, happily arguing about the proper place for the yet-to-be broom-closet. Should it go here, or on maturer thought, here? I would be filled with amazement at them, amazement not unmixed with pity. Poor old dears! Well, no doubt it was all right for them. They had nothing better to do.

Of course they had nothing better to do. Not in this world.

The pity is that the home which they built was no longer mine when I was old enough to appreciate it. However, to this day, when in dreams I am going home, it is to this home that I go, so in some queer adolescent way I must have dimly realized something of the significance of what they were up to.

It was amazing what happened to that barn, which to start out with was nothing more than a plain, old, foursquare, upper-New-York-State barn, pushed up against a hillside so that it was two stories high in front and only one behind, which architectural peculiarity gave it a certain air of being beleaguered, as though it were fighting with its back against the wall. It had no graces and few virtues except that it had been made originally of strong materials with honest workmanship. But now it received a new rakish roof, a circling of window boxes afroth with pink geraniums, a sassy balcony and in back, after Laura had had a long quiet conference with the earth and was informed by it of its requirements, which is always the way she finds out how to make a garden, the hillside was pushed back a few feet, leveled and paved and planted to make the most delicious little outdoor room imaginable.

It was as intimate and pretty as a pretty woman's bedroom, and as gay as a Christmas card. It always seemed to me that it was there waiting for the most delicious women in the world, women with flowerlike clothes and flowerlike manners, who surely were due to arrive at any moment, and that the flowers rooted in earth would then quite naturally bow in greeting to their human sisters, crisp as the geraniums, fresh as the rose petals and fragrant as the hyacinths. No one ever lived up to the setting, except perhaps Adelaide Hughes, for she was always like a scarlet tulip, and her hands could sketch the same lovely lines as a tulip bowing its head before the wind. She had a voice like husky honey, too.

Laura herself, who made the garden, never dressed up to

it. She was too busy grubbing in the earth all day and every day, just fair drunk with dirt and growth and the joy of turning up the earth. On her twenty-fifth wedding anniversary she was offered a silver tea service, but she took a carload of manure instead. She is a very great artist in the most wonderful materials in the world—manure being the chiefest of these—along with earth, rocks, trees, hills and the contours of the land itself. It seems to surprise her slightly when she is told this. Of course she is far from sane on the subject.

I have seen her, all eighty-two pounds of her, draped in pale pink brocade, cloaked in ermine and shod in satin, suddenly dart out of her car and back into her garden to attend to a plant which "didn't look happy." Once busied with the invalid's needs, she was quite oblivious of her grandeur, of time and of a waiting dinner party. When found and led back to the car all her pink and cream self was nostalgically tinged with a whiff of eau de fertilizer and her satin slippers gummed to the scuppers. She was sent upstairs to make herself clean and tidy and reappeared wearing an entirely phony look of contrition, phony because she was like a good biddable child who has just been rebuked for something which she does not consider a fault. She hopes to placate the grownups by pretending remorse, but as for her, *her* conscience is perfectly clear.

We had not been long installed in our rakish barn, when Dad went to the wars. He sailed away on a bitter cold morning in January, and Moie and I went down to the docks to see him off, and stood shivering there, though only half from cold, for a long time while his papers were scrutinized and his luggage got aboard. I remember the shock of seeing that his ship was camouflaged, and realizing that it was thus strangely striped and stippled because it was going into most perilous places, and with my father aboard it. Incredible! What monstrous sort of a world was this where my father, that source of all security, was going to be put in jeopardy? He made us laugh even then, though, by coming off the ship grinning at the spectacle he made in a life belt. "I sure boil over the top of this thing like a charlotte russe, don't I?" he asked.

He came home a year and more later, in July, and as he did not want us to worry about him being again on the dangerous seas he did not let us know that he was arriving. The first intimation that Laura had of his home-coming was when he telephoned her from the dock.

"Hello," he said. "Hello, Loll."

"Hello," said she. "Who is this?"

"Why, it's me," he said. "It's Irvin."

"Irvin who?" asked Laura.

"Your husband."

"I'm sorry," said Laura. "I'm afraid I don't understand who you are."

"Look here, woman," he roared. "Just how many Irvins are you married to anyhow?"

So then she dropped the receiver and began to weep with excitement and they were cut off and Dad could not get her back, but just went on up to Grand Central and caught a train to Ossining, still not sure whether his wife knew that he was home or not.

In the years that followed he worked hard and when I write hard I mean terribly hard. After all, everything, the whole accumulating mass of possessions, house, sixty acres, barns, horses, cars, cows, chickens—and houses for the chickens, but very seldom any eggs—gardens and their upkeep, tractors, furniture, and all the things that possessions lead one to, like parties, servants, trips, schools, debuts, country clubs, night clubs and investments to safeguard the future of the possessions, which in turn will forever, in a horrible, dizzy kind of interplay, require endless living up to—all that was supported and paid for by the short stories and articles he wrote. He never wrote a successsful play, nor garnered in much of that lovely movie money—not comparatively, that is. No, it was a new story, out of his head, month after month, year after year, that kept the whole glittering, spinning, whirling accumulation together. He used to say that he suffered from nightmares, that someday his head would stop working for him, and that it wasn't like a factory after all; it would not keep on producing for Papa, if Papa quit it.

Of course an income like his is not really an income at all, it is capital and should be regarded as such. Just the same it is very hard after years of privation not to spend most, if not all, of that green stuff with the Presidents' pictures on it, once it does start pouring in.

I have no intention in this book of discussing my father's work from a critical point of view. Indeed I am disqualified for that job for two reasons: I am his daughter and I am not a critic. I am writing about his work now only because of my immense admiration for the self-discipline that kept him at it, kept him producing, ill or well, until the very last days of his long, hard-working, generous life.

My father had twenty years and more of life before him, but everything that happened to him from now on had already happened before; they were pleasant years, most of them, but they held no surprises. Believe me, I am speaking without egotism when I say that the rest of the story is about me. It was my marriages that agitated him, not his own—his own had been attended to and was a working proposition; it was my babies who were the joy of his old age, not his. As everyone must, sooner or later, he began to live vicariously. I know all about this, for now it is so for me.

But they were pleasant years, good to remember.

Our house in East Hampton, which he told me that he liked better than any of the others, gave us all enormous pleasure, but he did not build that house as he had built "Rebel Ridge" in Ossining, nor struggle and plan and calculate, nor run into foolish expense, so, though he may have enjoyed it more, it was never really his very own, except on the title deeds, which is not what I am talking about.

He had a fine time at East Hampton in his own peculiar way, which was one to baffle and irritate his more conventional neighbors.

For instance he took up golf . . . at least he took up something which he elected to call golf and played it with the usual "tools" (his name for his clubs) on the Maidstone Links. It bore small resemblance to another game of the same name played by Mr. Bobby Jones, however.

As opponents in his game he gathered in Bobbie Appleton and Olga and Sidney Fish and me, and although I am not one to stickle (that's what a stickler does, is it not?) for too rigid adherence to the rules of any game, preferring a little give and take here and there, if it makes for fun, I must say that his, and Bobbie's, method of winning from each other was one that even I could not approve of. It was like this, as they played it: the man who won the hole was not necessarily the man who had struck the ball with the "tool" the fewest number of times. No—the man who won, in their contests, was the man who counted up his strokes last. For instance: Bobbie would ask "How many did you take, Irvin?"

And Irvin would say, "It's your turn to say first. How many did *you* take?"

"Ten. And you?"

"Nine."

"Why, you robber! I know you took eleven."

"So what?" Irvin would demand. "You were sucker enough to give your score first. My hole."

Catch on? The game was to make the other fellow commit himself . . . then you won that hole. The sport came in trying to confuse him so that he forgot whether or not it was his turn to lie.

Also, although I think it is perfect nonsense never to play a game unless your clothes are rigidly correct, I must admit that when the Fishes and Bobbie and Irvin sauntered forth to tear up that poor golf course their costumes were sometimes odd—not to say alarming. Why, I remember one day when Olga appeared wearing some very old knitted slacks which drooped most astonishingly in the rear. As she was suffering from a bad sunburn she carried a small parasol, handing this to her caddy when hitting the ball. Furthermore, she was towing behind her a small pup which had been recently afflicted with a slight paralysis of its hindquarters. The vet had told her that he would benefit greatly by regular exercise and certainly a walk around the golf links provided that. It had, however, no taste for sport; it preferred sitting down. Sidney had joined the group at the last moment, not bothering to change from his riding clothes, and said it was a wonder to him how hard it was to play eighteen holes in high boots. Bobbie Appleton, who'd liefer face a charging bull elephant than a small current of air, and has never been seen without at least two mufflers draped about his person, had decided that it was chilly that day and so must have been wearing at least six— we called him Bob Cratchit Appleton after Tiny Tim's father, also a muffler-fancier. And Irvin was wearing a white linen smock, a cowboy belt of silver and turquoise, and his city hat.

I tell you people fell into the bunkers and laughed so hard they did themselves mischiefs with the sand they swallowed!

But when they recovered themselves they went up to the clu
and complained to the Greens Committee.

That day, purely by accident, Dad hit a long, straight, low
miraculous shot, and landed on the green, and made a hole i
two. (Bobbie tried to take it away from him because it wa
his turn to lie about his score on that hole, and with a face o
brass claimed that *he* had made the hole in one, but after bein

threatened with a putter, was induced to withdraw his claim.
Always claimed he'd been gypped though.) Now no one could
possibly have been more surprised than Dad at that glorious
shot; indeed at the time he made it he had turned around to
say something to Olga, and it's my personal opinion that the
club slipped, and as he was trying to catch it, it came in contact
with the ball. We watched with open mouths that swift long

flight, straight and powerful, saw it falter, and sighed, saw it pick up a sudden little last spurt, rise in the air with a last supreme effort, fall and trickle onto the green, not three feet from the cup. And Dad turned to his caddy, as thunderstruck as any of us and feeling that someone besides himself must have been responsible, said, "Look, son, what's your mother's name and address? . . . I want to send her some flowers!"

Besides destroying the deep, deep peace of the links, those sacred groves and glades where it is a misdemeanor to smile and an impiety to laugh out loud, he greatly endeared himself to the inhabitants of the Hamptons in other ways: for instance, by making up little quips, jests and funny sayings, keeping these up his sleeve until he had gathered a few cronies about him, say some summer morning at the Phil Ruxtons' cabaña on the beach, and then springing them on what he was sure was an enchanted populace.

Well, maybe! . . . It might have done no harm if the jest had fallen only upon the ears of the chosen, but with his well-trained and very penetrating voice, if all and sundry lunching at the club that day did *not* hear him it was only because they had ventured forth without their ear trumpets, and were people requiring ear trumpets to hear anything whatsoever.

His most triumphant epigram was thus brought forth. I use the word triumphant because in a single sentence it names four separate communities, and manages to insult all four equally, and it is impossible to do better than that. Whether it was advisable or not—well, judge for yourself.

He said that the fact that there were such differences between the several Hamptons was most puzzling, all of them being small towns, nestling within a few miles of one another against the salt-sprayed breast of Long Island, and all catering to summer visitors from the same city, and yet it was well known that West Hamptonites wear Southamptonites' old clothes, that it

takes an athlete to keep *out* of East Hampton society, and tha
when a good Southamptonite dies he goes to Newport, but a
bad one spends eternity in Hampton Bays.

Well, we used to have happy summers down there—sorta
lonely after that but happy. Now these were the big boom
years, just before they went boom-boom, and the money that he
and Laura had confided to the nice man at the bank had grown
up into a tidy sum. It wasn't a cool million—in fact I've never
thought that a million *could* be cool—but it was in a fair
way to becoming a warm, not to say, hot million. So Irvin
began to take things a little easier and to talk of retiring. Definitely he was not going to renew his contract with the *Cosmo-
politan,* which required him to write a certain number of
stories and articles each year. He was going to take a good
long loaf and get all the fishing and hunting that his heart
craved. After that he might write a "little piece" every now
and then, as the spirit moved him. Just another year of the
stock market behaving itself and we'd see a guy starting the
vacation he'd been looking forward to since he was sixteen.
Yes, sir!

So we did not think that he had any marked talent for
loafing, did we? Listen! We were about to look upon a
gentleman so lazy that from now on he'd never so much as
uncross his own legs . . . not if he could hire anyone to do it
for him, we weren't!

That was in the fall of '29. And then one day the nice man
at the bank called up to say . . . Oh, well, everybody knows
what the nice man at the bank called up to say! For what the
N. M. at the B. said to him he was also saying to everyone
else in America.

I remember one gloomy Sunday in November when he
and I were taking a walk together. The last mile. That's what
we felt that promenade to be. A doomed processional. In the

morning the tumbrels would be pulling up at our door. Maybe they would not carry us to the actual guillotine, but we decided that on the whole we'd prefer to "kiss the widow" than live in the poorhouse.

The day before he had heard of the failure of the great investment house of Goldman Saks. Oh, yes . . . he was heavily involved. He walked silently for many miles. Finally he turned to me and said, "Well, this year I pay no income tax. . . . Thank you, Mr. Goldman—thank you, Mr. Saks!"

And then suddenly he could not write any more short stories. That was all there was to it. He did not have any more short stories left in his system. Perhaps he had so thoroughly convinced his subconscious that he was going to stop that some inner censor took over and would not permit him to continue, his subconscious either not knowing, or not caring, whether he was broke or not.

He did a radio show, he tinkered around, he was worried and unhappy and confused. And one fine day Hal Roach turned up with a suggestion that he come out to Hollywood and make some short pictures. A long correspondence ensued, with both of them writing firmly at cross purposes, as Irvin thought that he was to write the shorts and Hal wished him to act in them.

When this slight misunderstanding was cleared up Dad thought about the idea for a long time, hesitated, took the revolutionary notion off with him to his hole and lived with it, emerging from time to time to say that to save him he could not make up his mind.

He wasn't fooling me a bit. Two or three things came up about then that seemed to make a trip to the coast advisable. Will Rogers was about to make the picture *Judge Priest,* and I had sold a novel to Twentieth Century-Fox myself. It might be a pleasant little jaunt, if the two of us went out to see the process of bringing our brain children to life on the screer Did I think that a good idea? I said that I did. But I knew His going had nothing whatever to do with *Judge Priest,* muc less with my little darling (and I don't want to boast, and know there is many another who will protest the crown wit me, but I am convinced against all argument that that wa the worst picture ever made). He said he wanted the tri and the change, and the money. Nonsense! He wanted to ac

Chapter 5

No Holly in the Wood

WE were absolutely delighted with everything. Sunshine, palm trees (which was pure infatuation because in soberer moments we had long since decided that a palm tree is as tiresome, prickly, untidy, shadeless and monotonous a vegetable as any that grows on the fair face of the earth, particularly that commonest California variety which looks as though it were wearing dirty brown bloomers), people, architecture, the movie business, the Pacific Ocean, Derby hats to eat in and Ye Olde Gasoline Shoppe at which to buy our gas, actors, agents, everything. . . .

They opened the new post office in Beverly Hills while we were there, a handsome building and one to pridefully warm the cockles of the civic heart. We were staying at the Beverly-Wilshire Hotel and from our windows had an excellent view of the celebration which marked the event. Floats there were, and bands, and cute little tricks, done up in bandmasters' hats and twirling batons like all get out. Charming! Here was imagination. These people had a flair. Where else would one find a float heavy-laden with a group of scantily clad damsels throwing roses to delighted throngs, out enlivening the streets and pleasuring the pedestrians, and all in honor of a new post office?

One night we were invited to a big party down at the shore. On our way we passed the village of Westwood. We saw cloud-capped towers brightly illuminated, and fountains play-

ing and lights flashing across the sky, so naturally we called
out to the chauffeur to stop at once and let us take a good
look at these wonders. Indeed we were in half a mind to call
our hostess and say that we were unavoidably detained. There
was certainly a party going on right where we found ourselves
and probably a much better one than that to which we were
regretfully headed. What am I saying? Party! This was
more than a party . . . it was a fete, a festival. Surely behind
those exquisite light-wrapped towers there were fountains running with wine and a populace dancing in the streets. It
would be unpardonable to disappoint our hostess, of course,
but hadn't we better call her all the same and tell her what
was going on? Undoubtedly she would prefer to cancel her
dinner and bring her guests here instead.

The chauffeur stopped as directed, but seemed puzzled. He
hopped out and came around and opened the door and asked,
"Why do you want to stop here, Mr. Cobb? We've got plenty
of gas."

"Gas? What's gas got to do with it? We want to find out
why all those beautiful towers are lighted up. What are they
celebrating?"

"Towers? . . . Lighted up? . . . Celebrating? I don't get you."

"Why, use your eyes, man! There must be ten or more
towers—it looks like a California version of the towers of San
Gemignnano . . . with neon lights. . . . What goes on?"

"Why, these are gas stations. Nothing goes on—unless you
think we ought to buy some gas . . . whether we need it or
not."

At the party we attended that night I had a most fantastic
conversation with the gentleman who was told off to be my
dinner partner. I was not a bit surprised. I was expecting
things fantastic by now, getting to think like a real Californian
so that if everything wasn't fantastic . . . why, then it was fan-

:astic! We were dining in a most beautifully paneled room, hung with Gainsboroughs and Lawrences. At a discreet distance a string quartet made pleasant music. The guest of honor was an Episcopal bishop. Gary Cooper and Charles Boyer were there too, but the bishop, though not so pretty, was the star. My dinner partner was a young banker from Chicago and this was his first Hollywood party. He kept looking around in the most puzzled sort of way, and finally toward the end of a very long meal he could contain himself no longer. "Would you tell me something?" he asked in a discreet whisper. "Tell me . . . how soon does the orgy start?"

"Well," I said, "I haven't been in Hollywood very long, but I have attended several parties. And judging by them the orgy will start almost immediately after dinner."

His poor puzzled face relaxed, an expression of bright expectancy came over it.

"Really!" he breathed. "What will happen?"

"Our hostess," I said, "will divide the sheep from the goats. All the goats will be taken in one room, all the sheep in another."

"Yes, yes. Go on."

"And then," I said, "all the goats will play bridge, and all the sheep will look at a new movie. And at eleven o'clock, sheep and goats all together, we go home."

If that young man had had a gun he would have shot me through the heart. Nevertheless that is exactly what we did. That is exactly what we always did.

I stayed out on the coast only about six weeks that trip, and when I left my mother came out to join Dad. He was having a fine time, he loved Hal Roach and he loved making pictures, and his idea was that he and Laura rent a house for a few months and see how they liked living in the West. He was sick of New York and had a notion that this might be a pleasant place in which to settle. But on one thing was he adamant. They were not going to buy a house until they had given the place a long try. In fact he was not going to buy a house at all. They had bought too many houses as it was. And somehow whenever they bought a place it was the kind of place that no one else wanted. It was practically impossible for us to sell our houses; sometimes we even had difficulty in giving one away.

"Do you understand me, Loll?" he said. "We are not going to buy a house."

"Certainly I understand you. Besides I don't want to buy a house either."

"And if I send you out to look for one, you promise on your sacred word of honor that you will only rent it. On no conditions will you buy it?"

"But I've told you already——"

"All right, all right! . . . Now see if you can find us a house. And I don't want a house that looks like it had been built by a collaboration between Grover Cleveland and a Mexican day laborer either. None of this Early Hollywood Spanish, if you follow me. And I don't want it down at the bottom of a canyon or hanging on the side of a mountain. I'm no mountain goat. I'm not even a hillbilly. I like to walk around my garden without being forced to carry an alpenstock. And I don't want a big house. But I want one big enough so that Buff and the babies can come and visit. And I don't want enormous grounds—they are too much trouble and too expensive to keep up—but I do insist on absolute privacy. Now go and find it. But don't buy it."

As you can imagine, tracking down his dream house was a lengthy business. She was pretty near despair before she was through, for if she found a place possessing one of his qualifications it was inevitably lacking in another.

At last one day the real-estate agent, who was getting pretty tired himself, I dare say, drove her in through the evergreen gate of 1717 San Vicente Boulevard and she took one look and said, "But this is it! Why didn't you bring me here first thing and save us both all our trouble?"

"I knew this was the place you had been looking for," he said. "It meets every specification. There is only one catch. It is not for rent. It is for sale."

"Drive on," said Laura. "I'm not interested."

She met Irvin for lunch and told him what had happened. For a man who wasn't going to buy a house, he was strangely interested in her description. And after lunch, hemming and hawing a little, and looking sly, he suggested that they just run out and look at the house.

"But it is not for rent, Irvin."

"It can't do any harm just to look."

The very next morning he woke her up at a quarter past nine in the morning by throwing the deeds to the house onto her bed. He would have had them there earlier if the real-state office and the bank had opened before nine.

They wired me in New York what they had done and I replied with a loud wail; what did they mean by abandoning me like this, they were all the parents I had and only parents had no business acting like that. But the next winter my life worked up to one of its recurrent crises and then, oh, how grateful I was to be able to pack the kids and myself on the train and head for the sunset and my mother's house!

That was a trip! I was escorting two babies, a nurse, and a half-witted spaniel yclept Tipsy, who was stricken with such train fright that she wouldn't, or couldn't, wee-wee all the way from New York to Kansas City. No, she wasn't too well

housebroken, any such thing! At least if she were she re
spected the floor of the train a whole lot more than she eve
had my white rugs. Finally, on the platform in Kansas City
where I had escorted her, Tipsy gave. The kids were watching
from the window of the lower berth, being intensely anxiou:
about her, and no wonder, and how they clapped their little
hands, what joyous smiles lighted up their little faces and how
clearly and loudly they cried, "Oh, look, look! Everybody look
and see the beautiful puddle Tipsy's made!"

The nurse lost everything except herself (there'd have beer
some point to that), and Cobbie, escorted to Marshall Field':
to while away the time between trains, slipped, or was pushed
from the taxi and fell in the gutter which was a foot deep in
mud, slush, ice and the greasiest, stickiest, blackest gummux
I ever did see in any gutter, or on any small boy. At the time
he was sporting a pale blue outfit, leggings, bonnet and coat.
Of course it was a total loss, we resigned ourselves to that, but
what we never did get used to was the strong smell of he-goat
that pervaded the drawing room and which we tracked down
to his (formerly) blue suit. There was no difficulty in tracking
that smell either. One could have followed it across a desert
waste!

What I have never understood is: how did he get to smell
like that? It is so seldom that a herd of billy goats is tethered
in front of Marshall Field's.

Under the guise of friendship some fiend in human form had
given the children a large box of modeling clay, which I was
simple-minded enough to hand over to them, so that they
might amuse themselves on the train. They certainly did!
When we got to Pasadena they had to blast before they got
us dug out.

Oh, there is nothing like a trip with a baby who has tangled
with a goat, a suffering spaniel two inches thick in assorted

shades of modeling clay, and a nurse who has just remembered where she left her own personal feather bed.

When I got out or, more likely, crawled out of the car in front of the house and walked into that cool, fragrant, lovely flowering place, with Dad's arm around me and Moie crying out a welcome at the same moment that she was removing Cobb to wash him, I tell you I thought I had died and gone to heaven.

Maybe I had. But this I know: if heaven is like Hollywood you get awfully bored there.

It's the funniest thing. Why is one bored in Hollywood? I don't know. I only know that one is. Here is a beautiful climate, except of course for a few weeks in the rainy season when the rains come down, one's retaining wall goes down, and the termites fall in. Here is most gloriously lovely country, hills and canyons rolling and tumbling to a most dramatic suicide in a blue sea. Here are meadows dressed in tawny velvet trimmed with green. Here is.... Well, no doubt you too have read some of the publications of the Los Angeles Chamber of Commerce yourself. But somehow it never seemed to me to be real. I remember once standing on our back terrace which was as massed with bloom as a bridesmaid's bouquet, looking out across the canyon, most blessedly green because of a golf course set out there, and to the range of hills opposite, hills with a most lovely, suave line carrying them flying down to the sea.

"What's wrong with that view, Ivy?" I asked. "There's something.... It worries me."

"I know. It does me too." He reflected for a moment. "It is very beautiful and still.... Know what I think? ... It isn't real! ... I feel that if I cared to take the trouble I could have those hills moved about ten miles back, which would be perfect. It wouldn't be at all like moving one of the eternal hills

of God. I cannot imagine personally moving a mountain i
Virginia, or Maine. But these are—are just a backdrop. *A*
painted stage backdrop."

"Not a stage backdrop," I objected; "a movie backdrop. De
signed for Mr. Cecil B. DeMille."

"That's right: C. B. always does things in a big way. Wel
I know him. Someday I must ask him to attend to this littl
matter for me."

"I dunno," I said.

"You dunno what?"

"Dunno that C. B. will do you a favor."

"Why not?"

"Well, remember that job you were going to ask him for?

"I never asked C. B. DeMille for a job in my life."

"Come now! Think," I admonished him. "Remember whe
we were coming out here together the first time, and you rea
in the paper that Mr. De Mille was making *Cleopatra* wit
Claudette Colbert, and you wondered if he had cast the as
yet?"

"What are you talking about?"

"The asp—the snake that was concealed in the basket of fig
and was smuggled in to her and bit her bosom and she died?

"Oh! *that* asp—now if you're asping me . . ."

"Certainly that asp! On account you were so stuck o
Claudette, and you figured Mr. De Mille always did things i
such a big way that when he cast an asp it wouldn't be ju
any little old snake—it would be large and handsome. In fac
that you'd make absolutely an ideal asp. And would enjo
the work no little!"

"There is," said my father, "a certain irreverence prevalen
around these parts which I find but little to my liking," an
left me.

For the rest, the California climate would be the healthie

in the world, if everybody wasn't sick all the time. If you don't believe me just wait until your sinus trouble comes back with that new sun-kissed vigor!

And the people. Something happens to the people. We weren't in exile. We had plenty of friends, old ones who had preceded us, and new ones whom we grew to love. Exactly the same sort of friends we would have chosen for ourselves if we had never gone west of Jersey City (which is not a bad idea). We had friends in the movies, or of the movies, and some who were as detached from anything to do with the making of moving pictures and the people who do so as though they had lived in Chillicothe, Ohio, or London, England, instead of Beverly Hills. The only trouble was that all the folks we liked were so unhappy. Never in all my life have I heard so much grumbling and fussing and moaning and fretting as at an average dinner party given by Hollywoodians. Naturally the cute kids, male and female, who are snatched from behind a drugstore counter or out of a gas station and made into movie stars think it's wonderful, but I have noticed that even they perk up something wonderful when given a vacation and a ticket to New York. Lots of highly civilized and charming actor folk like living there, but poor darlings, that is because they have been "troupers" for so long that the bliss of settling in one place for more than a one-night stand goes to their heads. They can bring up their children and have a regular life, and I suppose no one in all this world so craves this as much as a professional wanderer. What they forget is that houses and lots and babies are wont to be had in other communities besides Hollywood. They confuse the issue. They think that they are adoring Hollywood, when what they are really adoring is their home life.

There have been a lot of beefs about Hollywood parties, and naturally these vary—good, bad and lousy—as where indeed

do they not? Personally I used to get a little fretful at the
big parties, not because they weren't beautifully and most
tastefully done, but because there was less mingling of the
sexes at a really big Hollywood binge than any other gather-
ings in history except Quaker meetings. I'm the old-fashioned
type. I like a man around the party. I remember Dad getting
all upset the first time he took me to a big shindig and found
me, after many hours, sitting in a room with nothing but
women. He knew that I had been there all evening and he
also felt that he had wasted a lot of money when he blew me
to that Irene dress. I hardly needed an Irene dress to wear
while talking obstetrics with a bunch of girls. (Of course we
talked obstetrics. That's topic A.)

And if anybody's got a rude comment to make here . . . let
me tell you that among the other wallflowers present that
evening were the three top glamour girls of the industry.

I also objected, strongly, but not nearly so strongly as he
did, to being invited to a buffet supper at quarter past seven
but never getting anything to eat until at least ten. One's
hostess always cooed, "You know we have to have such early
evenings out here because everybody works so hard and has
to get up at dawn." Well, that is perfectly true. And it is only
sensible and considerate that parties should both begin and
end at a reasonable hour. But that being so, why ask you so
early and feed you so late?

After two or three such experiences I caught on, and when
going alone used to fortify myself with a cup of soup and a
sandwich in my own room about seven-thirty. But Dad
being an old stalwart, and congenitally unable to be thirty
seconds late to any engagement, always insisted on arriving
precisely on the minute named. Sometimes, not often but
sometimes, the extra help engaged for the evening arrived
before us, and once we actually found our host downstairs

As he was wearing a sweat shirt and an harassed expression I thought that we had caught the poor wretch before he had had a chance to change for the evening, especially as his wife descended some forty minutes later dressed in pale pink brocade and rubies. However, as he changed neither expression nor shirt but remained as he was for the rest of the evening, I may have been wrong.

We found that it was best when attending the average buffet supper to take as escort a husband, a father, or at the very least a boy friend over whom you exercise an almost uncanny control. You see, at buffet supper all the married couples sit together at dinner. Always. Hence the atmosphere is so strongly domestic that an unattached male is liable to get a little nervous and abandon you for an instinctive drift toward the stags, of whom there are usually a smattering, clinging firmly to one another for reasons best known to themselves.

That's gospel. Married people in Hollywood almost always sit together, side by side, and at the same table at buffet suppers. My theory about this is that most of the marriages contracted hereabouts last such a short time that if people didn't sit together at parties they would never have time enough to get to know each other well enough to get a divorce.

I seem to be harping somewhat unduly on buffet suppers. Well, we went to such a lot of them.

Of course the segregation of the sexes is not so marked at cocktail parties. Cocktail parties are sexier. But as they inevitably wind up in buffet suppers . . . here we go again.

Incidentally we gave buffet suppers. They were just as bad as anybody else's, too. In fact once or twice I think we gave some particularly distinguished little horrors. For instance, the one where I got so tough about bullying the company into coming on time. Like this. Harry and Clare Boothe Luce were coming out, and as I had but recently spent something like six weeks as their guest it seemed only the sporting thing that I give them a little party when they came to my town. As Dad adored Clare he flung himself into the preparations with his whole heart.

It was his suggestion that for once we should be stern about the dinner hour. I was to call the guests and tell them that even though this was a buffet supper, we were inviting people at eight and would sit down at eight-thirty, and no nonsense about it, and if they could not make it, say so now because we were not going to wait for anybody. So there!

I must have thrown the fear of the Lord into our guests, for, wonder of wonders, out of a gathering of some forty people not one soul was late. It was a miracle, it was the marvel of the age.

A buffet supper, in Hollywood, all guests present, and served on time! Unheard of! Marvelous! How *did* we do it? . . . Well—we didn't!

For Irvin Cobb, as he descended for dinner (that lovely on-time dinner with all those docile and intimidated on-time guests) had paused briefly in the kitchen to ask Nan, our beloved cook, if she were serving some of her famous corn-bread sticks for dinner tonight. She said no, I had not ordered them, and he said, nonsense, she never thinks of anything, I want some corn-bread sticks, and swept on, affable and charming as all get out!

But there wasn't any corn meal in the house, so Nan got into her car and went to buy some, and the car broke down, and the first shop was closed, and she couldn't get a taxi, and with one thing and another she was gone over forty-five minutes, and as it takes some time to make corn-bread sticks, by that time the company, whom I had bullied and bribed and intimidated into being on time, was all utterly exhausted and worn out and had drunk too many cocktails out of pure fatigue, and the rest of dinner was ruined of course—not that anyone wanted it by that time. But we had corn-bread sticks.

And then there was the time that Jean Negulesco brought his newest girl friend to a party. That, too, was what you'd call a successful affair. I don't think! Jean had called to say he was madly in love with the most divine of creatures, and could he bring her? And I said sure, why not? and so he did.

And she was lovely, and a great addition. Then after supper he told me that she was not only all this but a singer too, and didn't I think it would be delightful if she sang for us? And I said indeed yes, but alas the only piano in the house was an upright in the nursery. "Think nothing of it," says Jean, holding affectionately to his lady's hand while she smiled sweetly in what I thought a most obliging manner. "I will enlist the services of some of the men, and we will carry the piano downstairs, and she will sing." And the young person smiled some more, and I said that it would indeed be a treat to have some music, and bustled off, putting the bite on this one and that one so that they would help carry down the piano. It was an upright piano, but it was not a small upright, and before those unfortunate men had maneuvered it down some very steep stairs, they had their coats off, and their tempers off too, and many was the sprained back and many the frayed disposition, and almost half an hour of exceedingly hard labor had passed. At last the piano stood ready, in the middle of the living-room floor. And then I turned to Jean's nightingale and said, "At last! We are all waiting to hear you."

And she said, "Who, me?"

And I said, "Yes, dear, you! You may not have noticed but some half-dozen men have just carried a large piano downstairs so that you might sing."

And she said, "But how odd of them! Everybody **knows** that I never sing after dinner."

Well, after that we thought we'd stop giving buffet dinners and concentrate on small intimate little parties like we used to have in New York. At the first one, to which twelve were bid, only five managed to turn up, letting us know at the very last minute. Now this was not their fault. They were all people working at studios, and no more masters of their own time than doctors are. Still it did put a slight crimp in the party. And of the five valiants who did arrive one had a sprained back from being required to fall off a wall nine times in one afternoon, and then the director was not satisfied and so he—oh shucks! why do I say "he"? Let's out with it— Basil Rathbone, for that's who it was, was left contemplating the joyous prospect of falling off that wall nine times again the next morning, if not oftener, and another guest, Florence Rice, was a little broody because she had to be at the studio at *five-thirty in the morning to have her hair washed!*

But undaunted we tried it again. The small dinner I mean. This time ten were invited. Fifteen came. Naturally no one dreamed that we'd be that silly again, so, thinking it was sure to be a buffet supper and wouldn't matter, they just brought along their current heartthrob, or agent, or somebody and didn't get enough to eat, which was some consolation.

And then there were the nights when I drove the car. Those nights it always rained. And I never could find the place where we were supposed to go. They make a very sporting proposition out of finding places in Hollywood anyhow, by always putting the name of the street on the opposite side of the road from where you are required to drive, and painting the number of the block on the gutters, and then letting fallen leaves and stuff accumulate there until the markings are quite obliterated or covered over. Many considerate people put the number of their house outside where it should be clearly visible even on a rainy night, but then almost invariably train a geranium vine to grow over it. Geraniums grow very quickly and most profusely in Southern California. There's nothing more fun than digging, in a thin evening frock, under a large wet geranium on a stormy night. Especially if it isn't the right geranium. And if you have followed this argument so far you will easily see how it very well might not be.

But the settlement called Bel-Air is the worst. Bel-Air, Irvin said, was laid out by a drunken angleworm. It wanders about a most unsymmetrical mountain, with every road running round and round biting its own tail, and, to make things just dandy, they change the names of these roads every now and then. Not for any particular reason. It's the same road as far as the uninitiated can see. It hasn't come to a place, or a stop, or an end to anything. No, it just gets its name changed, because whoever named the roads just naturally got tired of having the same old name around all the time. At least that's the only logical reason that I can think up for the system of nomenclature now in use in Bel-Air. Be that as it may, when I had to drive on a rainy night into Bel-Air I used to add to the equipment of the dashboard a large and reliable Ouija board. If ever a girl needed a spirit guide it was me. And there came such a night, and Dad and I set forth. Three times I went up the mountain called Bel-Air, and by three different routes, and three times wound up on the back side of that mountain, at a place where all roads stop, because there is no place for them to go from there, except into space, and the San Fernando Valley, some quarter of a mile below. Directly below. This is what is known as a jumping-off place. Which is certainly what I felt like doing the third time I fetched it!

There was only a tiny space in which to turn around, it was greasy and slippery under the car wheels, for a steady three-day rain had turned the road into slimy mud, and there was no railing between me and dear old San Fernando down, down below, so that when once again, and again, and again, I found myself in that perilous spot and faced with the necessity of inching that big heavy car around, with my poor arms and back aching from former efforts, I just gave in and put my head down on the wheel and frankly burst into tears.

Dad was most sympathetic, and maybe a little nervous. He said, "Now don't you cry, baby . . . we'll just stay here forever. Never mind if it is a trackless waste. We'll raise a flag and claim it for the United States!"

And then there were the many fancy-dress balls. And those I never did understand. I love a fancy-dress ball but that's because I get so tired of my same old puss and same old personality that a fancy-dress ball is a treat and a release for me. But these balls were given for, and by, *actors*. People who spend all day wearing heavy make-up and wigs and uncomfortable costumes. And then they take off their make-up and wig and costume, and go home tired, and put on a make-up and a wig and a costume, and go to a party! I don't get it.

But at one Dad and I had a most joyous moment, more than joyous, really colossal! From then on, whenever we wanted to imply that something was really of the Hollywood Hollywoody (as one says "of the earth earthy") we would look at each other and whisper, "Countess."

But I must tell the story.

We had gone to a fancy-dress ball, an enormous party, and at suppertime we found ourselves somewhat astray. So we were taken pity on by some comparative strangers who permitted us to join them. At the table was a ravishingly lovely foreigner, Countess Quelquechose, wearing, as this was a Spanish fancy-dress party, a black lace crinoline and mantilla. Her dress was very beautiful, and as she boasted lovely shoulders she had very wisely had it made strapless. She was having a fine time, and no wonder, but with one thing and another, the bit of black lace in the front, usually secured by something besides the wearer's person, had slipped, and a very great deal more of the Countess than she had bargained for was visible to

an avidly interested gathering. There was a great buzz going on among the other women about this.

"My dear . . . tell her."

"Oh, no, I couldn't—I don't know her well enough," and so on and so forth.

Sitting next to the Countess was a small man, eating his supper and paying her no mind, but finally he overheard the prattle of us girls and asked what was the matter. Somebody whispered to him and he said, "Oh, for Pete's sake! What's the matter with you women anyhow! I'll tell her." And he did. He leaned forward and said quietly, "Say, Countess, your tit's out."

Well, those were our gay days. . . . And then suddenly Irvin began not to feel so well and also to suffer some grave financial reverses, which meant that we must curtail our expenses, and that of course meant no more big parties. Hollywood is the easiest place in the world in which to drop out of sight. It is not that people there are less kindly than they are anywhere else, indeed I think that in many ways they are the most generous and thoughtful folk in the world, but they are terribly busy people and they live at great distances from one another. Somebody once called Los Angeles "Seven Suburbs in Search of a City." This geographical peculiarity does not make "dropping in on the chance" very feasible.

So we were more thrown in upon ourselves than at any time I can remember. It was a grand thing for the kids because they had so much more of their grandfather than they would have had otherwise. He was ever Cobbie's refuge, from the day shortly after his arrival in California when, suffering from some unendurable stress, he slipped into Dad's workroom, closed the door behind him and lifted up a tear-stained face to say, "My, it's nice here. Just us mens together!"

After that almost every afternoon Dad would tell him a bit of the saga of Cobbie Elephant. The stories always started the same, with Cobbie Elephant running away from Nanny Elephant and Mummy Elephant and going down into the canyon to see life, and there . . . Ah! And there the most awful things used to happen to poor Cobbie Elephant, while Cobbie Brody straddled his grandfather's knees, facing him and holding tighter and tighter to his lapels, his small body quivering with fearful ecstasy and his small face reduced to nothing but a pair of enormous eyes.

Once when Cobbie Elephant had tangled with a tiger called Leo Carrillo Tiger, it was too much. Cobbie Brody relaxed his clutch on Dad's lapel and fell backward, stiff as a chip, crying out, "No, Ivy—*no*, Ivy!" And then with a most wonderful and instantaneous recovery of courage assumed the falsest smile I ever saw and, turning over, galloped out of the room on all fours crying, "Who cares about a tiger? Here goes one—here's one now!" However, it was noticed that the instant he thought himself out of sight, he assumed an upright position and ran like the devil to Nanny.

Will Rogers did not live so very far from us, and that was a great place for Dad to wander of an afternoon and "visit a spell." It near killed him when Will went, and so soon after he had lost that other beloved Will—Will Hogg. It is nice to dream of a heaven where those who have loved one another may meet again. Dad's heaven will be a campfire in the woods, with Bob Davis getting the dinner, and he and the two Wills and O. O. McIntyre listening to Charley Russell tell stories. There will be no women on the premises. I think that he had a sufficiency of women down here.

There's no denying it, women do clutter up the place more than somewhat. I can remember with what relish he used to quote Freddie March's masseur who once said, "Know what happens soon as you marry a dame, Freddie? . . . No? . . . Well, they always got to get their teeth fixed. Always. There's no denying it . . . women bother people."

Or perhaps Dad will be quoting Cobbie instead: "My, it's nice here. Just us mens together!"

Dad took me to the Rogers ranch when we made that first trip together. It was a most glorious blue and gold spring day, and when Will came out to meet us, grinning that wonderful, inimitable grin of his, and stood there on the porch of his low-slung ranch house—and it really was a ranch house—I felt that he was giving us a welcome as big as he was, and there isn't anything bigger than that, and that here was a man as good as bread and butter and as rare as golden wine. I don't suppose there was anyone who ever met Will Rogers who didn't feel that way about him.

He was having quite a little party that day. O. O. and May-belle McIntyre were there, and Mr. and Mrs. Will Hays and Billie Burke, and Will Rogers, under the mistaken notion that the troupe required more entertainment than he could provide all by himself, had ordered out a new buckboard—his heart's darling—hitched up a pair of mules and announced that he was going to drive us into the canyon where he had just had a rough road cut out of the hills.

We all piled in, a full load of us, and started out accompanied by a most picturesque cowboy person in full regalia on a high-spirited horse. When Will played Wild West, which has its difficulties in suburban Hollywood with a polo field and a "drive-in" not half a mile away, he did the thing up brown. In fact that afternoon he came near doing it up so brown that he all but cooked our goose (or should it be geese?), for on our way home as we were coming down the steep mountain trail, which was barely wide enough for the buckboard, some gadget on the harness broke, the buckboard slid forward and hit the mules a smart lick on their hinderparts, upon which they put their ears back and without further ado most enthusiastically ran away.

I was sitting in the backmost back seat and did not realize what was happening, or that we were in more than considerable danger until I heard Dad drawl, "Look here, Will Rogers, if you're going to spill this contraption, would you mind spilling it on the side where the actors are sitting, thus sparing English literature an irreparable loss?"

Then Billie Burke, who sure enough was sitting on the opposite side from Dad and Odd screamed, "Don't you listen to a word that man says, Will!"

At that moment my part of the buckboard swung clear out into space, and then I swear that blessed cowboy galloped off the path into thin air, somehow swung his horse back onto the path, was alongside the flying mule team, had leaped from his horse onto the back of the nearest one and was sawing so savagely at its mouth that that mule began to see reason, and reflect himself and slow up.

We all behaved very well. We even made quite a few little jokes, saying that we knew all the time that Will had staged the runaway on purpose because he was so stuck on getting a little realism into his Western act. But it was pretty feeble jesting. We were all honestly scared to death.

It was just about this time that Dad received a blow from which I think that he never recovered. Of course it was dealt him by a friend. No mere enemy can hurt as badly.

He had been writing a daily column, a fine thing for his morale and his pocketbook, and had thought that it was doing pretty well. But the man in the syndicate who handled his stuff wrote him that it wasn't and would have to be discontinued. It was a nice enough letter, and no reason it should not have been as it was from an old friend. Dad was sorry about it, sick sorry indeed, but he blamed nobody except himself. He would have felt better maybe if he could have put the onus of his failure on someone else, but he didn't. He was most forlorn, though, so Laura packed him off for a little trip to San Francisco, the town that was for him ever renewer of delights and city of comrades.

While he was away I acted as his secretary, opening and answering his business mail, and so one morning I found myself reading a letter from the editor of a paper in the Middle West who, although a stranger to my father, yet had sympathy enough and kindness enough to write and tell him that he was sorry the column was being discontinued and that he failed to see why the syndicate's announcement of its cancellation was so curt and summary. He enclosed a copy of the syndicate's letter. Curt indeed! It was crushing. When I thought of all the successful work Dad had given to the syndicate, of all the friends he had there, the letter made me first sick and then furious. There is no law compelling even a small shred of generosity but plenty of people give it away in large quantities. Not, it would seem, whoever wrote this letter; he hewed right to the line and let the chips fall regardless.

Well, I wrote the Middle Western editor telling him he must accept my thanks in place of my father's for I never wanted him to know about the syndicate's announcement. And then I passed a happy week writing letters to the syndicate, telling them just what I thought of them. I took my time and wrote and rewrote and my typewriter was oiled with wrath. I was gradually evolving a letter that would have raised blisters on the soul. But Laura, who was maybe madder even than I was, said what was the use because this syndicate didn't have a soul to raise blisters on.

So I put away the letters I had written, and the editor's from the Midwest, and the syndicate's announcement, because I was still brooding on what to do about them. A few weeks later Dad came prowling around when I was out, looking for paper or stamps or such, and found them. The syndicate letter nearly killed him.

Well, after that, we who had been the gay, mad Cobbs really did become that old hermit family down on San Vicente.

Every now and then we'd rouse ourselves and go out to see how wagged the world, but mostly we stayed behind the hedge and barked at unwary visitors. Dad began to have a hard time filling in the hours, that dreariest of all pursuits. He was feeling so bad that he could not work very long at a time, though even so he did manage to write a quarter-million words of autobiography.

Then his doctors put him on a diet. Aha! That's what they thought! The simple plain food that he required was prepared for him, all right; getting him to eat it was another matter. He absolutely refused to believe that a lamp chop and a baked potato smothered in assorted pickles, pepper sauce, fresh-ground black pepper, A-1 sauce, barbecue sauce, vinegar and a few other dabs of assorted condiments was not just as good for him as though left in a state of nature. In fact he had quite made up his mind that anything he liked was good for him, and what he liked would blister the insides of a chameleon. I remember once he went off for a little expedition to Leo Carrillo's ranch and came back with a monumental stomach-ache about which he made much moan, saying that he guessed he was a goner this time, for no matter what he ate or how careful he was, he kept on getting these bad upsets. Suspiciously we asked him what he had been eating and he said, "Nothing at all, not one blessed thing except some G. D. slops."

Then Leo dropped by to inquire how Ivy was feeling, saying that he had been afraid that the two quarts of peanuts and popcorn with molasses that he had consumed during the trip might have upset him some.

After that, although we continued to minister, it was with considerably less sympathy. Indeed, he said that our attitude was both harsh and unfeeling, particularly mine, but this was when he recovered enough to crave food and I offered him milk toast and tea instead of country-cured sausages and fried apples, and he a sick man and a helpless and just plain old pining for some honest victuals with a taste to them.

Sick or well, the days passed slowly for him now. He would work for an hour or two in the morning, but as he always woke with the dawn, when none but a few belated, inhuman night prowlers were abroad in the land, this left him with a long, long day stretching before him. He would putter around with his Indian stuff for a while, and then ... then there was nothing to do.

In New York he would have company in his clubs, but out on the Coast the only clubs geographically available were for golfers, and now that he did not have Bobby and Olga and Sidney to play his way he had lost what little enthusiasm he had ever possessed for the game. Once we coaxed him into going to the races at Santa Anita, but he did not enjoy himself very much. He said that every time he bet on a horse it always remembered where it had left its umbrella and went back to look.

I was working then and was liable to get home late. It used to strike me to the heart to see that always he had waited for his afternoon toddy until I arrived to share it with him. He did not care about the drink. He cared about the sociability. While we drank it he would repeat to me, if I had missed it, the highlights from the broadcast of a certain news commentator that used to come to us 'long about first-drink time. This gentleman was far from a favorite with him. In fact he detested him, his views, his diction, his voice. So much so, indeed, that he used to look forward with the greatest excitement to the hour of the broadcast, so that he could have the pleasure of detesting him all over again. Brisk as a button he was, while this gentleman held forth—"Old God-aw-Mighty's Ghost Writer," he called him—and he'd greet me with pleased chuckles, "Well, the official Gloomy Gus of the air waves had a bum time this afternoon. . . . Seems the news is good, and that most broke his heart. You know, the day we win this war I bet Jeremiah with a Microphone cries himself to death!"

Occasionally we would lure him out to dinner, but he always came home as soon as possible to prop himself in bed and read detective stories. Only once did we get him to accompany the family to the movies. And of course that night luck would have it they were showing the worst picture I ever saw, with the exception of mine. He said he'd be willing to wager quite a handsome sum that the picture had been smuggled out of the studio, that some dirty dog with a grudge against the producer had picked it up off the cutting-room floor and rushed it to this theater, and just as soon as it was discovered that this thing had been actually shown to an innocent and unsuspecting audience that the police would step in. Or still better, the Marines. In that case, everybody concerned would face a firing squad.

And then, to make the evening complete, he mislaid his new store teeth. It seems that he had slyly withdrawn them during the performance, and tucked them in his pocket. Or that's what he thought. It was dark when we came out, and all of us were slightly stupefied with the effects of the picture, so that none of us noticed he was as toothless as an angleworm, or that his face, sans denture, was folded up like an accordion. We had reached home, and he gave the usual little grunt that accompanied the effort of climbing out of his seat, and the grunt came out a lisp! Startled at his own personal sound effects, he reached guiltily for his teeth. And they were gone.

During the subsequent uproar he maintained an air of aloof dignity, refusing to accept the blame. It was not his fault. He explained that he had grown so bored and restless during the movie that he had become conscious of his new teeth for the first time and in an impulsive moment had taken them out. If he had not been so miserable—and through no fault of his own—he would have hung onto his teeth, and his sanity. Before he got through shifting the blame for his loss onto me, who had urged the expedition, and Moie, who had backed me up, he pinned it onto the studio that had made the picture and was about ready to sue Darryl Zanuck or Sam Goldwyn or Louis B. Mayer, or whatever criminal was responsible for the double outrage.

Laura said, "Oh, hush now, Irvin, do!" and went to call the theater, and there an excited manager assured her that indeed, yes, they would start a search immediately. No, it did not matter at all that the picture was still going on. They would dispatch ushers with flashlights at once, even if it did mean disturbing the audience. They seemed to feel it was of the utmost importance that those teeth be found. One can see what they meant. After all, they might very well have been reposing in all their glory on a seat, waiting, ready, coiled to strike, and if somebody, in all innocence and confidence, started to sit down—a person of a nervous temperament, say—the consequences might be alarming.

But the teeth were not found that night. Toothless and peaceful, he slept. Next morning a cleaning woman unearthed them from where they had been carefully tucked, down in the crack between the arm of the chair and the seat. This lady immediately gave notice. She said she had found some mighty odd things while cleaning up that theater, but those teeth were the last straw. Enough is enough, and when that turns out to be a set of Cobb teeth—we all being equipped with originals ample for a large lion or a small horse—enough is too much.

The Willkie campaign came along about then, and Dad started off to the campaign (under strict orders to keep his teeth in and on his person). Dark misgivings at the propriety of his working for a Republican were besetting him, and he was only reconciled at all because a great many other folk who felt as he did were permitted to call themselves "Democrats for Willkie." If that slogan had not been devised he would never have gone, although if a third term had been put over without his voice being raised, and heard, in opposition to it, I verily believe he would have died there and then from ingrowing eloquence, which is just as fatal as the measles when they "turn in."

It was a great time for him. He was proud and glad to be called on for this service, always granting that it was understood he was a Democrat—born, bred, sweating, fighting, old-line and Jeffersonian. I think that he knew this was the last time he could go out and fight for what he believed in, the last time he could stand up and fight as a citizen for the rights of citizenship. He was always a good citizen, in a large way when the opportunity offered itself, as it was doing now, or in a small one, for he never lived in any town that he was not part of all those community efforts of which he approved. He worked for the Children's Village in New York, for the hospital in Ossining, for the local charities in East Hampton, for the Community Chest in Santa Monica, for the Salvation Army everywhere. There were lots of others; we never knew how many until the letters came to tell us after his death.

But this time he was not going out only as a good citizen doing his bounden duty. For him this was a crusade.

His big night came in Oklahoma City at a mammoth rally. That night he was put on a national hook-up, which naturally pleased him, as proof that what he had to say was thought worthy of being heard by the whole country. Also, this was Will Rogers' town and part of that West he loved better than any place in the world with, of course, the exception of Paducah, Kentucky.

There was only one place in town big enough to hold the crowd, and that was the big arena where they hold the stock shows, and Dad told me that when he arrived and found that his car was to enter through one of the chutes usually used for cattle, he said, "Why not? They're still going to get a lot of bull."

They waited outside the chute for the signal to enter at the right minute, there being some canny showmanship displayed by the committee—and there a little old bent darky kept hovering around, unobtrusive but very evident, in that wonderful and mysterious Afro-American manner. He was armed with a broom and a badge, so it was apparent that he had been hired for the occasion, and Dad said that if he had not been born down South he might even have imagined that the old man was actually doing some work. Looking mighty busy and preoccupied, he would stir up a little trash, and leave it, then stir up a little more, always edging nearer and nearer the official car. Finally he got close enough so that he could be heard when he murmured as though to himself that he certainly would like to hear Mr. Cobb speak tonight, he certainly would, particularly as he was a Republican his ownself. This remark was, of course, not addressed to anyone in particular. If it happened to fall on interested, and powerful, ears, why, who more surprised than he?

Dad called him over to the car. "Look here, Uncle," he said, that being his old-fashioned and courteous way of addressing any older person of color, "you can hear the speeches, and see the show if you want to. It's free. It's for all people. You go right on in and get yourself a seat."

"No, suh," said the old man. "They's no section for colored people, and I don't aim to make no trouble."

It seemed then as though things had come to an impasse, but as the old man still lingered, making play with his broom and some nonexistent trash, Dad knew that a proposition was coming up. "But, suh," said the old man, as Dad had known he would, "I was one of the ones helped make that little pulpit for you—" he meant the rostrum—"and right under where you is goin' to speak they is two, three little old scantlin' boards. . . . Effen I could git out there, I bustle under the platform and hang onto 'em. . . . Wouldn't be nobody see me— wouldn't nobody know I was there even—'n' then I could see the show . . . effen I could figure some way to git out there."

"All right," said Dad. "Hang onto the running board of the car when we go in, and then you duck on under the platform. But listen to me, if I hear a sound out of you after we go on the air, I'll skin you alive. Hear me?"

The big tra-ra-ra came then, they shot in through the chute to the sound of the band. As the song crashed out, the lights flared and some thousands of people rose and shouted in the good old political-rally way, Dad forgot all about the old man. There was a preliminary speech or two, and then Dad's turn. Being a reasonably canny showman in his own right, he started his speech with a sort of invocation, or if you look at it another way, a tribute to Will Rogers, and as this was his home town, even if all that enormous crowd were not going out to vote Republican when Election Day came, still all of them could be counted on to holler their heads off at anything reasonably complimentary about their boy. Will Rogers was what you might call right popular in his own home town. While the crowd still roared, Dad got the signal that he was on the air, braced himself a little, took firm hold of the speaker's rostrum and got ready to turn himself loose on a listening world. And then without any warning at all, a little old black head rose up from under his feet until it was all but in his lap. It was Uncle, rearing up from his uncertain perch on the "scantlin' boards" to say, "Uh! Uh! . . . You and me kin stop right now, Boss! . . . Oklahoma done gone Republican!"

I was listening to that speech in a parked car out on the desert near Palm Springs, California, and I heard Dad say, "Ladies——" and then sort of stop and choke, and I grabbed Betty Fox in a panic, thinking that something had happened to him—and then he pulled himself together and in a firmer voice repeated, "Ladies and Gentlemen," and I knew he was all right. Incidentally so was his speech. It was a scorcher.

When he got back from that trip I asked him what had put him off just as he was swinging into the best talk he'd ever made, and he told me about Uncle. He said that first this black apparition suddenly appearing practically in his lap almost scared him to death, second his remark fetched up such a laugh that swallowing it all but choked him, and thirdly he was overcome with an intense desire to take a scantlin' board and beat Uncle senseless.

I was in New York the Sunday of Pearl Harbor, and so missed the first excited days of the war when all California feared, and with good reason, that at any moment a Japanese army might move in to join their relatives who had already preceded them. I am referring to the beetles here, of course. Irvin and Laura seemed to be among the few that remained perfectly calm and went quietly about their business. Dad wrote me, "Your mother has provided us with some sand with which to put out incendiary bombs, goes to the Red Cross to roll bandages, I'm trying to get into any outfit that will have me and if none of them will, we'll just stay here, and if the Japs do come, well, I'm not a bad bird shot and before they get me maybe I can contrive to send one or two small yellow rats on ahead of me."

Later on he wrote me a letter that seemed an odd mixture of pride and exasperation concerning Laura's conduct the night they had the big scare in Los Angeles when some unidentified plane, or planes, went over the city and all the antiaircraft batteries opened up and blasted the innocent heavens. He said that the guns woke him up, and as one who had been there before he knew at once what that sound meant, so he got up and went into Moie's room in case she was nervous. She was not only not nervous, she was not even awake. However, his entrance did rouse her and she asked in considerable alarm if there were anything the matter with him.

"I'm all right," he said. "I only thought you might like to know that we are being bombed—or at least that we may be at any moment."

"Oh," said Laura, "is there anything that I can do?"

"Well, not anything that I can think of right now."

"In that case," said Laura, "I think I will go back to sleep." And so she did. Dad said that there was no question but that my mother was a hardheaded, stubborn, contrary, opinionated little thing, but also one had to admit that she was a true Liberty County Baker, and they ever a sandy breed.

He finally chuckled himself to sleep remembering the old story about Laura's ancestor, Colonel John Baker, who having seen some service in the Indian wars, was elected commander of a volunteer outfit which was happily anticipating a little trouble with the English. Incidentally, at the siege of Charleston, they got it. Colonel John called his first drill, lined up his men, all of them old planter pals, and gave his first command like this: "Gentlemen of the Liberty County Guards, you will kindly come to attention."

I went out to the Coast again that spring and found that we were landed in a big house surrounded by a bigger garden and, surprise! surprise!—that we had no servants. Moie was nearly working herself down to her chassis trying to keep the garden partly alive, Dad was miserably ill, Pat was sick with an obscure glandular fever, Cobbie didn't look any too well—and I was cook. I didn't mind being cook—in fact, I am like the guy who had never played the violin. I had always thought I might be good if I ever tried. I still think so, but somehow my family don't seem to encourage me much. Well, anyhow, I'm better than I was. Now I can light the oven without first sending for the fire department.

The first morning that I was to get breakfast Dad woke me early, at least it seemed early to me although he had waited in the most angelic fashion until almost seven o'clock, which was practically midday to him. At that hour I make even less sense than usual unless gently plied with coffee made by somebody else, but I staggered down to the kitchen full of the best intentions and a lot of leftover sleep.

But I woke right up at the sight of the stove—a great black inimical piece of ironmongery with its works as dark a mystery to me as though it were a bank vault. Awake or dreaming I didn't know how to light that thing. The top burners yielded their secret without doing anything worse than singeing off my eyebrows, but the oven—— Ah! the oven! I opened little doors, and then I quickly closed them again. I didn't like the look of those grim caverns at all. All the Liberty County Baker drained right out of me. I approached my poor, patient, hungry Pa.

"Dad," said I, "will you light the oven for me?" "Who, me?" he asked.

"Well, unless we wait for the mailman—and he doesn't usually get here until about ten o'clock—there isn't anybody else," I explained.

"Any ass can light an oven," he said.

"In that case, light it," said I.

He got up and followed me into the kitchen, where we stood

hand in hand for a long time looking sadly at the gloomy cold stove. "Baby," he said, "I'd just as lief try and tame Siegfried's dragon as that thing."

"I'd liefer," I told him.

He sighed. "One of us should have learned something useful," he said. "I guess it should have been me."

I began to laugh, and then to cry a little, because that broke me up so, and he patted me on the back and said to manage as best I could. The best I could turned out to be hard-boiled scrambled eggs, bacon that could have been tied into true lovers' knots, and some perfectly lovely fried toast. And he ate it.

Naturally our house did not retain its pristine shininess, although Moie did yeoman service, always choosing the toughest, meanest jobs for herself. Indeed, it got so that when we missed her, we automatically went out to the incinerator to see if she was cleaning it again. She almost always was.

Finally, one afternoon, Dad wandered out onto the terrace and surveyed his domain with a sad eye. "Come on out here, women," he commanded. "This place looks like the kennel of the Hound of the Baskervilles. Let's clean her up."

He dug me out of the kitchen and the batter in which I was perpetually incased during those days—I could have been fried like a nice potato at any moment without any added grease—excavated Laura from out the ashes—"Cinderella, Cinderella, you shall go to the ball"—routed Pat and Cobbie from their respective hidey-holes, armed us with rakes and brooms, and then—imagine the audacity of him—was about to return to the contemplative life, when loud outcry from his family shamed him into taking a hand in the big cleanup. He grunted a little, but gave in, and once having decided to help was most eloquent and bossy.

"Little more elbow grease there, Buff," he would cry. "Hurry with those leaves now, Pat," and "Look alive now, Son." He had us trotting like ants until Pat, pausing to get her poor young breath, called out, "Why, Ivy! You haven't done a thing!"

We all stopped and looked at him. He was standing in a small circle of leaves and from time to time he would put out his rake and gently move one from one side of him to the other. He never actively molested 'em; he just stirred 'em up a trifle. "Tut," he said, "I'm more the executive type."

When we had finished our, and his, work, he called us together. "Now you women go on upstairs and pretty yourselves up," he commanded. "I'm sick of seeing you look like a road-company *Tobacco Road*. Especially you, Lolly. . . . Haven't you still got anything nice? With ruffles maybe?" She low'd as she guessed so and started in the house to do his bidding while he called after her, "And put on some perfume, too. Lots of perfume, the expensive kind."

That night we made a little fiesta. Pat got down the good plates and lighted the candles and fixed flowers and hors d'oeuvres, and I did my darnedest not to burn the dinner, or scorch it, or send it in lukewarm and half-cooked. He dressed too, in a brand, spanking, fresh, white smock and ice-cream pants, and as he stepped out into the patio to pick himself a flower—he always had a special bed of red and orange flowers suitable for boutonnieres—he said so wistfully, "I like this. I like to look at pretty women, sitting at a pretty table, with silver and lace and nice china. I like a party about once a week, and I like lots of doings to go with it."

I was so surprised. I had never known that. I knew that he was sociable and hospitable, but I had never guessed that he cared anything at all for the trappings. In fact, if I had thought about it at all, I would have surmised that he considered such things mere frippery and certainly not worth the money or the trouble. "Why, Ivy," I said, "then you've liked the way your home has been, haven't you? The things that mean so much to Moie and me are your cup of tea after all?"

"Of course," he said. "You don't think I'd stick around here with you females if I didn't like it, do you?"

I have always been so glad that he said that to me.

Shortly after that he got much sicker. So sick. In body, and I think in mind. Things were closing in on him somehow, and this man who had been a liberal—politically, intellectually, socially—drew back and sheered away from the convictions of a lifetime. He was suddenly a tory. And very lonely.

It always seems to me a strange thing that so often the self-made man becomes the great reactionary, frightened that the world he knew, and in which he was able to make his mark, should ever change. Perhaps all successful men are egotists, must be egotists, are required to be egotists—and so they cannot abide the idea of a world which they cannot dominate, and as they are no longer young enough to learn how to dominate this new one they both hate and fear it. I don't know if that is so, although I think it is. I do know how unhappy he was, and how fretted with a life that was no longer harmonious, no longer in tune with time.

The friends were good to him. Leo Carrillo would be over, bursting in with that smile to charm the birds from the boughs, or Margery and Madrena Duggan bringing him a treat, or Blanche and George Fournoy happening by to cheer him by laughing their heads off with him, or Roland Young driving the snappiest car in town, of which he always seems slightly intimidated, and all set to go through their usual ritual—which consisted of Roland telling Irvin darky stories, worse than darky stories have ever been told by mortal man, and Irvin telling Roland cockney stories, ditto. Bless them all, they were wonderful.

We had one more holiday. We went together to Arizona and New Mexico, and with him I saw the country that fascinated him above all others. And we laughed together there, like the good comrades we had always been.

I remember . . . Ruth and John Quirk and Dad and I are driving together once again to Witter Bynner's house (Witter Bynner, the poet, who gave us an evening to remember always). And suddenly, as we roll along, Dad says, "I've got a little thing drifting round my head . . . nice little thing, but I can't get on with it. Brilliant, really! . . . Only there's no finish."

So we ask him what, and he says, oh, all right, he'll tell us, and maybe we can help him with it. "It's a poem about our host," he explains. "As far as it goes, it goes like this:

" 'Mercy me!' said Witter Bynner,
        'Hasn't it been a bitter winter?' "

Ah me! I'm glad we had that trip together. I am so very glad.

He had a good time, too, and came home all afire, all over again, with the beauties and magic of his spiritual home from home, the great Southwest. While thus incandescent, he put on his cowboy hat and his silver harness, polished up his best tommy-hawk, and using it as a pen—or so I like to think—wrote the following "piece"—his last one.

"ME VERSUS THE LADY FROM PATERSON

Regardless of what I now propose to say about it, you might not care for Rainbow Bridge or what comes before you get there. You might be like the lady from Paterson.

The lady from Paterson eased her car down a screw-thread trail into the awesome gorge at Lee's Ferry. That's where Buck Lowery and Mrs. Buck lived in the shadows of the Vermillion Cliffs which some people, including artists, think are perhaps the most exquisitely tinted things that lie outdoors. Her license plates were dimmed with alkali dust and stained by mica grit of various mesas. She was accompanied by a small squashed gentleman who looked, so Buck claimed, exactly like a husband, and was moreover wearing a made tie.

"I hadn't seen a made tie in years," said Buck afterward. "You know—the kind that fastens on with a gadget, something like the latch on a backhouse door. Out here you couldn't even sell 'em to the Indians. From beginning to end he never spoke a word. Undoubtedly a husband.

"Well, she pulled up in front of this trading post and the first thing she said was 'Say, listen, how long is it going to take me to get out of all this red mess?' She didn't say 'us,' she said 'me,' if you get the drift.

"So I said, 'Lady, that all depends. Which direction did you come from and where're you heading for?'

"'From the Coast,' she says, 'and going home to Paterson, New Jersey, thank goodness!' Well, that left us both up a stump. Because it meant, getting back this far, she'd had to run along the Virgin River, and it all bordered on the upper side with steep red bluffs running up some several thousand feet in the air; and then through Zion Park which nobody can deny is likewise pretty well littered up with red, not to mention forty or fifty other shades. And after that, when she'd coasted off the Kanab Plateau, she struck into this-here real

honest-to-goodness auburn stuff which, under one name or another and with only a few breaks in between, circulates all the
way from away up in Utah on past this crossing and clean
across Arizona and doesn't start petering out on you until
you're good and well east of Gallup, over in New Mexico.
What's more, if I routed her out of here straight to Flagstaff,
she couldn't help but skirt the Painted Desert country which
is plenty red when not white or purple or blue or green or
buff or a mix-up of all such. And if she swung off along the
South Rim and out by Williams, she'd bump into a large section of absolutely unimproved real estate called the Grand
Canyon, the same being replete with sizeable rocks that are
pinkish, not to say reddish.

"So I said, 'Ma'am, I'm sorry to tell you, but no matter which
road you travel—and there's only the one road out of this
present obnoxious hollow for quite a spell—you're bound to be
annoyed by a lot of loose landscape. I reckon for the next five
or six hundred miles you'll just have to grit your teeth and
regret it. . . . I could sell you a pair of extra-dark smoked
glasses out of this store—they'll maybe help mitigate the dis-
tressfulness.'

"She gave me a square-jawed look and drove on," con-
cluded Buck. "I'll bet her sufferings must have been intense
till she was fully halfway back to her native Jersey where the
prevalent places never get red in the face and rear up in the
aggravating habit that they have around these parts."

With me the foregoing evidence was purely hearsay,
although Buck was known to be a truthful citizen and a
courteous one, out of Georgia originally but fotched up in
Texas. Even so, I feel reasonably sure the embittered lady from
Paterson would be seriously antagonized by Rainbow Bridge
and environs because that's where Old Marster stacked it up and
scooped it out and shuffled it together again so violently, so

completely and with such incredibly beautiful tonings, such inconceivable results in the finished article. Or anyhow so it would seem to one who, during these past thirty years, has done his share of prowling through the continental magicland which reaches its peaks of fantastic perfection on and near the Colorado River.

Of all the natural wonders in North America, Rainbow Bridge was the latest to be discovered, with the sole exception of Maligne Lake, as I mentioned a few pages back. It isn't because of the brief time lapse since then that fewer human eyes have looked upon it than upon any other of our national monuments or forest reserves or any of our national parks. It's because of the approach to it—a tricky approach which measurably could be abated by the expenditure for trail-work and highway-work or just a few thousands of the dollars which Uncle Sam so profusely slathered about, hither and yon, during those carefree and spendiferous years following the depression. I claim it would be money well spent. I state this from the depths of a being that was made painfully saddle-sore at the locality where a being gets the saddle-sorest. They call these high-pommeled leather contraptions Western stock saddles. They should be called chafing dishes.

To be historical about it, it was not until 1909 that a party under the distinguished archaeological explorer, Professor Byron Cummings, accompanied by John Wetherill, famous pathfinder, and guided by a Piute Indian, penetrated through a most difficult and scrambled-up-together terrain to what the Navajos, who knew it for centuries before these inquisitive white folks came limping in, called Tsay-Nun-Na-Ah, meaning "Where the Rock Goes across the Water."

And how the rock does go across the water! From Bridge Canyon Creek it rears, this rock, to a height of three hundred and nine feet and it has a span of two hundred and seventy-eight feet, being forty feet thick at the top, and its arch could swing entirely over the Capitol at Washington and still leave clearance for a band of New Deal congressmen to turn happy handsprings on the dome. There is an abundance of other figures touching on its general formation and its specific proportions, if you care for figures. In a case like this I am one who does not. For this is not a mathematical proposition; this is not even geological or geographical, unless you want to be technical about it. It is sheer cosmic poetry. Statistics, however sizable, just seem to curl up to insignificance when they start wriggling against a master achievement of the Divine Artificer—a creation so gorgeously symmetrical, so overwhelmingly majestic in itself, and so starkly splendid in its setting that the English language just lies down and begs for help when you try to picture it. I know this—the very first sight of it repaid for every new-laid blister upon my own setting and that, I may state for the benefit of any interested blister-fancier, means right smart setting.

Through months of occasional forays into the back spaces of Hopiland and of Navajoland, which surrounds it—trips to the ancient lost cities of Betatakin and Keet Seel, to the ruins beyond Chin Le, to the entry into Monument Valley, to remote trading posts where the aloof northern Navajos come to peddle their wares—piñon nuts and wool and goat hair and woven robes and hand-hammered silver set with turquoise— for the white man's gear and the white man's provender, we'd been promising ourselves that sometime soon we would gird our loins for the harder trek to Rainbow Bridge, farther up than we'd yet been, and across the state line. We knew the infinity of strange compositions which is the Arizona anteroom to this yet more marvelous formation. We'd bunked with Johnnie O'Farrell at Red Lake and seen a dramatic sun come up and dye the world a rich hot crimson. On the way to

Kayenta or Kai Bito, we had skirted White Mesa which is mainly white to prove its right to its name, but also pink in spots, and in the crannies a bright and burning coral, like a red-flannel mountain somewhat faded in the wash and bleached out still paler on the line. Half a dozen times we'd ridden, as we were now about to do again, between the columnar Elephant's Feet, those twin oddities of erosion that are complete even to the ankle joints of the monster and the toenails. It's a badly disassociated monster, for on this journey we were to find an authentic rump in one place and an indubitable head in another, miles away—scattered pieces of the same vast and preposterous jigsaw puzzle.

Anyhow came, as the fancy writers say, a day; a day when two of us—Buck Weaver and I—lit out from Flagstaff via Cameron and Tuba City and across the foot of Moenkapi Wash and past the head of Blue Canyon which is in some lights blue, and in others any color you'd care to think of. Good roads—that is, good as desert roads go, which means you won't mind them in dry weather, but would do well to travel with a rescue crew when it's wet—went with us all the weaving distance to Inscription House Post, which, literally, is the jumping-off place for the main attraction. From now on, scenically speaking, I'm sure it's going to keep on being the main attraction of the entire Western Hemisphere for me. I took the thirty-third degree in the lodge when I stood under that perfect rainbow which is frozen into everlasting stone, and looked up above me and looked round about me and testified before my Lord.

Except by a roundabout pack-train trip requiring several days, you couldn't reach the Bridge from the southern side at all, had it not been for the optimism of a rather public-spirited individual. You couldn't possibly reach it from any other quarter, either, unless you traveled upstream of that treacherous and turbulent river, the Colorado, from Lee's Ferry until you came to the mouth of Bridge Canyon Creek and then pushed inland through the savage canyon for seven of the roughest, crookedest miles imaginable. I don't know how many tourists have gone in by that waterway, if any, but whenever they are organizing such an expedition someone may have my place. Bucking against the old Colorado's justly celebrated current while half a mile down in the gash, between the sheer harsh palisades of one of the grimmest chasms on earth, would not be my idea of getting the most, in relaxation and peaceful contemplation of nature's devious moods, out of my next vacation. I'll take the Albany night boat.

Some sixteen or seventeen years ago, with the aid of Navajos who scouted the most feasible route for him, Hubert Richardson, the trader at Cameron, laid out the short cut, the one we followed. It's no boulevard, you understand. Not dangerous, either, but the car that makes the run must be part antelope and part roller coaster. The motives of Mr. Richardson were not altogether altruistic and yet, I'd say, not altogether selfish. To be sure he hoped—still hopes, I guess—to make the undertaking pay. He maintains the automobile connections in from civilization, and he owns and operates Rainbow Lodge at the limits of vehicular travel, and for a price he provides the hardy soul who has adventured thus far with pilotage and equipment for the last fourteen-mile stretch which twists and winds by mule track up and down most lofty inclines to the spot where the bridge is. But he is a benefactor in that through his enterprise the journey materially has been shortened and the going somewhat made easier and, most of all, the pathway opened wider for those who are willing to accept certain inevitable small hardships and handicaps for the rewards, in spiritual uplift and physical grandeur, awaiting them at the farther end. So when, once this war is over, if only the National Park Service boys or maybe it's the Forest Service boys—my! how the departmental bureaus do pile up and overlap these days— could get together with the Indian Bureau lads on the project of an engineered road to replace the present haphazard one and then add on a job of trail-smoothing, thousands of visitors would follow along, I'm betting, where heretofore there have been but scanty handfuls. Those who visited the place would become walking advertisements to fetch in the multitudes.

For us, the overture number proved worthy of the finished production. For two hours and for thirty-five miles we rode in that machine which had a bounding chamois for its mother. Sometimes we scooted through thickets of nut pine and juniper but mostly we inched along a narrowed rocky spine which rears up a mile and better above ocean level to separate Navajo Canyon from Piute Canyon, both being formidable sisters to Grand Canyon. There were periods, as we traversed that crooked spinal column of the Divide, when we could look down, this side, into the convoluted mysteries of Piute and, that side, across a breath-taking void upon the even more daunting panorama of Navajo, which is an experience not exactly to be duplicated anywhere else so far as I know, and, as already stated, this subscriber has been about quite a bit, off the beaten tracks. To the swales between Piute's bare ribs some of the Indians come with their flocks for shelter in the winter, but mighty few of them hibernate down in Navajo because there is where the ghosts of the "Other People" abide and the head devils of tribal demonology talk back and forth in the haunted nighttime. In the lower recesses of Navajo Canyon are said to be two hundred separate ruins of the cliff dwellers—probably more than that since the bewildering multiplicity of these rugged wall pockets forbids a complete census. From the jutted lip of the overhang far above, you can make out the squares and triangles of the dropping terraces that these industrious ancients, centuries and centuries ago, built with infinite labor into the steep flanges beneath their fortresslike homesites and their pyramided townsites—stair-step plots which, in the growing time for the melons and the maize and the wild peaches, must have been veritable hanging gardens of bright green against that grim and desolate scope of naked stone. You even can trace the zigzag lines of their tiny irrigation ditches leading from small spring holes. So this is why the ethnological sharps from the colleges and the museums dance with joy on the verges before they crawl down toward the defiles, there to delve and dig and dispute and frame contradictory theories touching on the lives, works and general conversation of these earliest American families who, like true Americans, put up the first skyscrapers of four, five and even six stories, and who utterly are vanished unless the Hopis and some of the Pueblo groups of today be their transmogrified descendants, as some contend. But others say no. Because your true scientist is a scientist who is absolutely sure that, other than himself, there are no true scientists, and therefore all the rest just naturally have to be wrong.

Anywhere in this, the real frontier of the Southwestern reservation country, you probably will encounter more relics of the aborigine races than sights of their modern kinfolks. In almost every hidden fold of the rumpled hills, or behind almost any stubby butte striking up from the sagebrush and the mesquite, it's likely there will be a daub-an-wattle hogan and a herd and a household, but these shy residents mainly shift away from the trading posts, adhering to their native beliefs and, insofar as contact with us has not yet altered them, following the nomadic impulses of their forefathers. Up under Navajo Mountain is probably the only spot left in the United States where, spring and fall, the bow and arrow regularly are used in killing small game. And they do say that away back off the road here are grownup Indians who never saw half a dozen white people in their lives—and found that amply sufficient and now they don't care if they never see any more white people the longest day they live.

It was at the lodge perched well up on the front of Navajo Moutain that we arrived in the cool of a flawless evening, so finishing the first extended lap of the expedition. Most mountains here occur in groups, like clutches of mottled eggs, but this giantess—she lacks a little of being 10,500 feet tall—as viewed from the southerly approach, soars up all by herself out of a comparatively flattish tableland straddling the state line between Utah and Arizona. On her haunches and behind her, toward the north, is where the girdling slopes jag off into one enormous oblong; an Olympian commingling of terrifying sheer drops and distorted upheavals and all manner of cavernous holes and corridors—perhaps the roughest, wildest, most disordered conglomerate in a territory which nowhere and never is what you would exactly call docile.

We bedded, upon clean, sweet-smelling sheets, in snug cabins. First though, we supped in a cozy main camp that fairly strutted its stuff—easy chairs and big open fireplaces and even an alcove where, luxuriously, you could take a hot shower, which we certainly did. So between ourselves we called this haven Bath and the austere, empty country behind us Beersheba. It's really astonishing how lightheaded a fellow gets in these high altitudes.

Next morning when hospitable Mrs. Bill Wilson had baited us on a filling breakfast and Mr. Bill, husband of above, had loaded and diamond-hitched the pack animals, I was introduced to Coyote, a rectangular mule of old-fashioned architecture, having numerous gables and a chastely severe southern exposure. Also he had a habit, as I soon found out, of halting on some eight-inch shelf and bunching all four of his feet together and then stretching his forward parts, where I precariously adhered, out over practically a bottomless abyss and, with a rapt expression on his fiddle-shaped face which would put you in mind of Mr. W. R. Hearst in one of his more pensive moods, stay there a spell—the sight-seeing so-and-so! During the ensuing two days we were often to feel each other's presence—Coyote and I. But I felt his presence more than he felt mine, I'm sure. This was not altogether due to his gait, which was easy as a mule's gait goes; nor altogether because of the up-and-down footing; nor even owing to Coyote's double mansard and his amusing dormers. Not for many months had I bestraddled a mount of any sort, and a lot of usually dependable leg muscles had gone soft and flabby. That mainly explains why for upward of a week I walked all spraddled out like a pair of calipers and flinched away from hard-bottomed benches. I'm afraid poor old Coyote forever after will have a permanent dip or sway approximately 'midships of where his early Colonial roof line meets the ambient sky line. And reflecting back upon the more outstanding of his personal experiences, I'm sure he must think I belonged to a strange tribe having a language of but three words and each a word of but one syllable, to wit: *Whoa! Ouch! Damn!*

Not ten minutes off the shaly ledge upon which the lodge sits and we realized that yesterday's ride along the top shelf of the great declivity, tipping out toward the desert levels, had been merely the prelude to what today was bringing us. We skirted a nubbin of First Canyon, so called, the trail wreathing through a fine pine growth, and turned a corner alongside which a gray pinnacle towered aloft like the Empire State Building, and involuntarily halted, held under spell by what revealed itself to our eyes.

It is agreed, I take it, that Grand Canyon as sighted either from Grand View or El Tovar is, despite its freakishness of composition or perhaps partly because of that very freak-ishness, the incomparable spectacle of both the Americas. And what a place to throw your old radio commentators!

Neither in the Canadian Rockies, nor in the High Sierras, nor even in the Andes, has this onlooker ever beheld aught to match it, let alone surpass it. For shift and play of color, for size, for balanced grouping, for weird modeling it convincingly is the hemisphere's supremest masterpiece. Creation made the Grand Canyon and then threw away the mold. I hear tell the Himalayas also dish up some very sightly stuff, but they'll have to show me.

Admitted all this to be true, I nevertheless bear witness that the fourteen-mile mule jaunt to Rainbow Bridge—considering what lies along the way and what theatrically awaits the trav-eler at the farther end—furnished me with more thrills per square yard than ever I have garnered in a like space anytime, anywhere.

By contrast, the Grand Canyon has been made convenient for the tourist. An air-conditioned train fetches you to El Tovar's doors. You may sit on an easy couch and peer over its brim at the immensities below, knowing there is a luxu-rious hotel at your rear and that tourist camps and lunch stands are near by and a paved thoroughfare leads either way along the edge. But to see the Rainbow you must cross about as rude a stretch of wilderness as is left in this country and brave some mighty brooding solitudes. And these adventures, even when negotiated with no special amount of danger, give the greenhorn a Daniel-Booneish satisfaction—the comforting thought of having earned his pleasure by undergoing travail and pioneering hardships.

Another difference is that the Grand Canyon lies open to the observer's eye. From above its major secrets are all readable. But here in this tangle of depths off Navajo Mountain is an endless spectacle which never fully betrays itself; which tantalizes you with faraway glimpses at obstacles humanly unconquerable, with unattainable elevations which you know can never be reduced to dimensional tables by some prying surveyor's squad. Take, for instance, Forbidden Canyon. Or take Wild Horse Mesa.

You have angled across a narrowed V at the head of First Canyon into Second Canyon and out again and are about to invade Third Canyon as a preliminary to traversing Cliff Canyon (I trust the reader is not getting confused) and thence through Redbud Pass to Bridge Canyon—as I say, you've reached Second Canyon when all of a sudden you come on Forbidden Canyon—and then perhaps an hour farther you ride out of a pent-in side draw which is a sort of hyphen connecting two infinitely larger gaps and are face to face with Wild Horse Mesa. At this range of vision Wild Horse Mesa looms like an unscalable back fence enclosing the myriad of unearthly glories which spread across the intervening dip. Close by and beneath you are varied formations—funnels and spirals and carved monoliths and, among and between these, curious wormlike arroyos, all changing, though, to faint clumps and shallow furrows where they lose shape and vaguely merge together away off yonder under the farthermost panels of runneled sandstone.

This noble barrier, with its base in the blended shadows and its top palings in the clouds, is so called because stray mustangs that have gone wilder than any deer are said to frequent it—which is more than puny mankind has done, although there are those who claimed to have climbed to the crest, going up an exceedingly precipitous ramp on the farther side. Well, maybe.

But until we develop sucker disks on our feet and learn to cling to smooth outbulging surfaces like houseflies crawling on finger bowls, I'm reasonably sure none of our species will ever get down into Forbidden Canyon or, having got down there, ever get out again. So you see it also is appropriately named. Were it not that bandings of sunshine and cloud play splash it with shifting pastel hues—dun, ecru, soft brown, blush-pink, dulled lavender—what lies cupped in there would be like a giant paint bucket scraped clean. It's the sensational coloring that makes the pageantry. Otherwise, the desolation would be so complete, the utter wastefulness of it all so depressing that you could imagine anyone who for very long stared down into that dreary pit going sick at the stomach. Birds fly above it but it is reasonably certain no living creature, anyway no two-footed or four-footed creature, exists in it.

Now most canyons pinch in like hourglasses. Usually they seem quite sheer until you draw near enough to note that there are vents like chimney flues in the outjutting rock crops at the crest and that these manholes lead down into weather-eaten seams and crannies by which a very nimble and clear-headed person may eventually reach the seemingly inaccessible bottom. But here these amazing walls all conform to a peculiar pattern, and form an endless succession of great, slick, convex shapes, offering no footholds even to a mountain goat, separated from one another by longitudinal clefts, and preserving a remarkable uniformity in their drab gray surfacing and their design. The most massive of these globular collops curved directly toward me from beyond a wide gap, or perhaps its comparative proximity made it seem larger than its fellows to the right and the left of it. I caught myself wondering what that vast rounded thing reminded me of. Was it a Cyclopean gourd gone gray with antiquity? Or a captive balloon everlastingly tethered and turned solid? No, something else; the clue was in my brain, yet eluded me. The answer came when, four miles deeper in, Bill Wilson halted the train to show us Elephant's Head Rock, that enormous and most cunningly chiseled phenomenon which, having been copiously photographed and reproduced, has done so much for the souvenir-postcard business at the Santa Fe's lunch stands back along the railroad. Here, miraculously thrown up in the bas-relief, was the front of a tired old circus performer, her lean skull outlined as clean as a cameo, her tuskless jaws loosely agape, her trunk dangling, her venerable rheumy eyes bedded deep in the scored wrinkles of eternal age and only the two ears less shrewdly etched than the rest. Why, of course, those were her dismembered feet which I had passed yesterday, propped in the tawny sands near Red Lake; and that gross rotundity which earlier today I had beheld in Forbidden Canyon would be the pachydermic posterior. There was no mistaking it. She certainly got herself widely distributed, that old lady.

We had started at 6,400 feet above sea level, and when we got through we had dropped off nearly 4,000 feet. At the upper extremity of Cliff Canyon was where we negotiated a considerable part of this dropping-off process, with a grade averaging almost thirty percent—and if, afoot, you should tackle a glacis any steeper than thirty percent, you'd practically be leaning backward. It would be a job, really, for the daring boys of Hook & Ladder Truck No. 7. Doing it mule-back, though, is the way to get the thrills. Here was where that confirmed student of landscape effects, namely, Coyote, had some of his biggest moments. But not his harassed rider. If this writer is expected to pay any compliments to Bridge Canyon, he would merely say that it's one of the best places in the world to lean up against.

We took the incredible plunge in one fell swoop, so to speak. Before we took off we didn't for the life of us see how we were going to slide down and, when we were down, we couldn't see how we were ever going to scale back up—an illusion which occurs on peaks less altitudinous than this. If I, for one, hadn't been so busy draping myself like the trailing arbutus on the gaunt trellises of Coyote's upper framework, I probably would have taken more interest in the fact that in this single operation we descended from the tall timber, through stunted and spiny desert growths, and on to the aspens and willows and cottonwoods of a better-watered level. It was with almost a shock of surprise that eventually I discovered myself still aboard Coyote's walking beams and Coyote ambling along a gentled swale. A nice chuckling little creek was marching with us and gossipy small springs clucked under the grassy banks. The noonday heat was baking fine resinous smells out of juniper and sage and sweet herbs and the Mormon tea bush. And along with whole plantations of flaunting sago lilies and gay cactus blooms and other big, pushy, brilliant things, the scallops of the slopes wore patchments of bright yellow stuff, and many wide troughs of white sand were flounced thick with such tender, shy flowers as you'd expect to find in your grandmother's garden instead of here, flanked in by these bleak guardian masses.

But, oh, such a lonesome spot and, oh, how silent except when we ourselves broke the hush and then the echoes barked like dogs! A mule shoe striking a pebble was as the clash of smitten cymbals. Call aloud and through the shattered quiet the sound boomeranged back to you, and pounded against your eardrums, a dozen times repeated. We saw no bobcat tracks nor tracks of the little dwarf rabbits in the moistened soil along the stream; it is claimed that no one traveling by night in this enclosure ever yet heard a hunkered coyote confessing his sins to the unresponsive moon. Even the swift little lizards and the overgrown insects of the high buttes were missing. Away off somewhere we did hear one cactus wren chirp to itself twice and then stop as though abashed; and a single strayed piñon jay called once. Then he quit, too. And that was all. We detected ourselves talking in half-whispers.

At its farther end Cliff Canyon appears to butt smack into an escarpment of solid mountain. You are right up against it almost before you see that, from top to bottom, this seeming barricade is split by a rift hardly wider than the foot trail which pierces it. This is the famous Redbud Pass. Verily, it's like the Crack of Doom made usable. There are places where your outstretched fingers brush both sides and, looking up out of the perpetual twilight of the bottom, the sky is seen only as a tiny blue strip. You have the feeling that any moment the crevice may close shut and flatten you like a bug caught between two book ends.

We had just entered this cleft when all of a sudden up came one of those impulsive thunderstorms of the tall country. It came with no warning and ended the same way but, while it prevailed, brought lashing of big fat raindrops and a lavish amount of lightning and contrariwise gusts that caromed off the cliffs and brutally whipped the cottonwoods and redbud bushes, and whistled shrilly past us for the right of way. Being inside by now we escaped the downpour, but to us, buried in that dim alley, the wind, slanting by, was the wailing of a lost banshee. Overhead and straight up the bolts skittered, and bounced off the craggy rim and left behind a sulfurous taint. And the thunderclaps, though somewhat muffled, kept reverberating and growling and drumming until one of us, calling back or forward to the others, had to strain his voice to be heard above that insane clamor. We could have asked for no more stirring curtain raiser to the impending climax. After that—and those mad orchestral effects—the last act just had to be good, which, verily, I say unto you, it was indeed, and then more and yet some.

As miners might emerge from a mine working, we issued

forth, numbed and deafened and thrilled to our several marrows, and immediately were confronted by a descent, not so prolonged as the aforesaid one in Cliff Canyon—merely a matter of three hundred feet or so, but most fabulously steep, in fact, as you might say, just straight up and down. A "horse-ladder" is what they call such things out in the trail country, it being fashioned of logs set in the earth for the mules to brace their hoofs on, and wedged down at either tip under boulders.

I said to myself that no mule born of a mare could climb down that preposterous staircase, but these mules made it without a bobble and, what's more, on the return trip next day clambered back up. They make it often, and always without mishap. When they die monuments should be erected in their memory.

Going down, they practically stood on their heads and where the cross rungs were far apart, coasted, each time to fetch up, just when I figured all was lost, with a hair-raising jolt against the next toe holt. Coyote and I were following Bill on the lead mule. Between Coyote's ears I looked straight down—or so it seemed to my popped eyes—at the back end of his mule, and my one consoling thought was that if Coyote missed connections and we did tumble, we'd take Bill and his mule along with us and probably have something softer than stone to light on at the bottom. It is difficult to avoid being selfish in a situation such as this. At an inopportune moment a hind foot of Bill's mule picked up a cup custard of freshly wetted earth and flung it back. I say inopportune because at the moment our cruppers were bumping together with painful emphasis—that is, my personal crupper was coming down on Coyote's leather-covered one; and I had my mouth ajar to moan, for when I moans, I moans! And that muddy gob took me right square in the face and spattered ever'-which-way. I must say this is not a very tasty mountain. Otherwise I have no criticism to offer.

Along the slanting path through Bridge Canyon we followed the creek which, having tunneled out of some subterranean channel at Redbud Pass, now had grown to a widened clear stream, full of deep pools; and the trees were taller and bushier than anywhere else on the route, and so deep were the wild grasses that the trail was a half-hidden trace, and a shepherdless flock of Navajo sheep found the richest of pasturage as they browsed about, led by an old ewe. She had a copper bell at her throatlatch and in that solitude the bell's jangling could be heard for half a mile before we saw her.

Divers curious indentations worn by the weathers of a million years high upon the canyon's tan-colored mural made a fascinating side show here. Yonder would be a squared doorway lintel, sill and jambs all complete; and just over there a tall unfinished archway, and next along a titanic picture frame but no picture to go in it. And then perhaps a funnel or a swirl, a cockle, an arabesque or an amazing rosette, like a pastrycook's decoration for some exaggerated caramel cake.

It was late in the afternoon and I was trying to sort out and classify for future reference a thousand different impressions, when we came to where the path forked. Right in the crotch was thrust up a smallish pone-shaped butte, heavily corrugated. Beyond the wrinkled withers of this dumpy lozenge we could catch a tempting peep at the nearmost pediment of the Bridge, but Bill advised that first we get to camp and rub the cramps out of ourselves and then return and go past another little elbow in the gulch for a view of the thing in its entirety. So we turned right-wing and presently butted into a blind alley where the swoop of a future cave formed a half-moon above a sweet spring pouring out of the rock; with a brush arbor and a corral and a storehouse handy by, and two wall tents with cots and mattresses in them and, crowning paradox for so untamed a vicinity, clean sheets for the beds and clean pillowcases for the pillows.

It's forty minutes later and the daylight is starting to fade on the lower shorings of the encompassing cliffs and I, being dismounted, am noting that I hurt in a lot of places where I hadn't hurt before, when we hobble stiffly beyond that interposing jog to a proper vantage point facing into the west—and now, mister, hush up your mouth and please just lemme pause and contemplate!

Already I have confessed total inability to describe what to me is the crowning achievement of the huge arena of uplifting magic in which it lies hidden. I shan't even try. I'd go downright delirious, whereas, at this date, thinking back and reliving that experience when I stood and soaked up pure loveliness through all my pores, I merely became semihysterical.

But I do crave the reader's kind indulgence while briefly I draw in retrospect some sketchy notion of that amphitheater where Rainbow Bridge is tossed up, a perfect symphony in pink sandstone, to unfold like a scroll thwartwise of the canyon's structure which, by contrast, is streaked with less graphic tones—umber and amber and ocher and bronze and tarnished brass. But with no vain ornamentations to mar the surpassing grace of it, mind you; no superfluous curlicues to distract the fascinated eye from those altogether simple and most truly scaled lines.

Except for the prodigality of coloring in which it is bathed there is a planned economy in every detail of the magnificent conception. And down below and beneath that splendid arching sweep, the little brawling creek hustles along, now riffling over its pygmy rapids and now boring between yellowish fringes that are polka-dotted with circular splotches of bright verdure. And on under and beyond the arch, the sun goes

down in a welter of unutterably brilliant cloud rack that is all
crumpled and strewn like torn remnants of silk flung across
the sky.

So in a kind of trance, a thralldom of happy catalepsy, while
the inadequate tongue had frozen but the soul was quickened
and the brain alert to absorb more and yet more of the beauties
of it, I bided there until twilight made everything blurred,
then dazedly stumbled away in the dusk, tripping over boulders and splashing through brisk eddies. It was just before the
last of the sunset that the glory became almost too glorious to
be borne. As the final benedictory rays played over the horizon
and struck upon the upper reaches of the great span, what a
moment before had been rufous, like a pochard drake's head,
now flamed scarlet, like a tanager's breast; and mauve turned
to royal purple, and palish green was emerald and dead gray
was all of a sudden opalescent and gleaming like the throats
of doves. A steep mica bed on the parent cliff alongside picked
up a slanted beam and became a cascade of diamonds; the
broken canyon floor lit up like a friendly hearth of ruddy fire-
bricks. And yonder through the crescent of the Bridge the
heavens flared with flamings of crimson and with waves of
blue and of tattered gold—God Almighty's housewarming.

But I'll bet you a purty the lady from Paterson wouldn't
care for it."

There were a few more laughs, much cherished and quoted
now—there was the night when we were dining with Hope
and Bud Leighton and poor Dad was so miserable, because
of having a tooth pulled that afternoon, that after taking one
Old Fashioned he withdrew into his dress shirt like a turtle into
its shell, nor emerged for the entire evening except to make
one, just one, remark. But it was *the* most outrageous remark
anybody ever made, and on that I'll take my oath. After that

my mother and I took him home—nor stood upon the order of our taking! Of course the instant we were safely in the car Laura turned to him, crying, "Irvin! How could you have said such a thing?"

He reflected and then he said, "I don't know. It is incredible. I cannot believe I said it. Even at the moment I didn't think it was me. It seemed to me that somebody else *must* have been using my voice!"

How did I live all the years without that excuse, which isn't really an excuse, but a profound truth? There are times in everybody's life, I am sure, when somebody else uses one's voice, and that somebody else is invariably a low-minded, impudent scoundrel.

It was about then that he wrote the following little piece— I think he had a lot of fun with this one, although it seems sort of grim fun to me now.

"Auto-Obituary

Word has been received from the old mesa of Walpi in Subsection 4 of Federalized Administrative Area 17-B (formerly northern Arizona) of the passing of Irvin S. Cobb, once fairly well known as a native writer. He was celebrating his one hundredth birthday when, attempting to cross his legs, unaided, he burst a blood vessel and died without a struggle.

Nine years ago, following the installation of Supreme Generalissimo "Buzzie" Dall, this venerable man helped to organize the few surviving members of the early stocks, both white and red, who abandoned the more abundant life and sought refuge in the battered stone-and-adobe huts which still adorn the semiarid expanses of Reclamation Scheme 1001. Cobb was among the last of the original founders—the self-styled conservatives.

With the tiresomeness frequently characteristic of the aged, he attributed his longevity—when he could corner a reluctant listener—to eating inordinately, smoking immoderately, drinking whatever he fancied whenever he fancied it, rarely taking any exercise, except once in a while to knock on wood, and making a habit of perspiring, gently but firmly, during hot weather. After his eightieth birthday his eyesight failed, but he smiled and said it didn't matter as there were very few things worth seeing that he hadn't seen. Similarly when deafness overtook him he declared that it was no grievous affliction since he could still appreciate his own remarks without being bored by the other fellow's.

Mr. Cobb left the request that his remains be cremated and the ashes enclosed in an old-style wooden cigar box, provided such an obsolete container could be found, and forwarded for burial to his birthplace in the extreme western part of South-Central Area 4-J. To the very end he cherished a senile vanity that his faded memory might be perpetuated in this locality, his claims being that he was ever a loyal son if no other kind, and that in his early works, now forgotten, he brought some small measure of fame—transient but not unpleasant—to the old town.

The burden of his frequent complaint was that from time to time in bygone years the suggestion had been volunteered that a schoolhouse, a park, or even a comfort station be given title in his honor but either through popular indifference or popular opposition, the project always failed. With almost his expiring breath, he is reported to have gasped: "Now my name will at last be on something permanent back home—on my tombstone." He further directed that the only other inscription on the slab should be the date of his death, with the words: "Well, anyway, he left here!"

However, it appears that this posthumous desire will probably not be realized. His descendants, while numerous, are widely scattered, some being on permanent relief and others employed upon various governmental projects and therefore difficult to find. Moreover, he left no belongings except some tattered manuscripts, and a collection of faded steel engravings of such primitive and discredited figures as Thomas Jefferson, Andrew Jackson and Abraham Lincoln, which, naturally, are now without intrinsic value.

It was due to a certain innate stubbornness that he died without assets. With a weak persistence he refused to accept the old-age pension of $1,800 a month in nationalized script, amounting, even at present rates, to approximately $72.50. This was allotted to him under the amended Townsend-Coughlin-Frankfurter Act, more generally known as the Pot-of-Gold-at-the-Foot-of-Every-Rainbow Plan.

It would indeed seem that most of the dreams of his career, if one might call it that, were thwarted. To begin with, as he often bitterly declared, he was cheated at the very baptismal font. The first intention was to christen him Joshua, after his father. But because of the sentimental insistence of certain female relatives he was labeled "Irvin." As he himself frequently put it, he didn't look in the least like an Irvin but did look a good deal like a Josh.

His adolescent aim was to be a cartoonist, but a change in the family fortunes forced him to deliver newspapers, which he did, though not brilliantly; then to drive an ice wagon, but showed no special aptitude, being inclined to day-doze while the stock melted. At eighteen, however, he found himself the youngest managing editor of a daily newspaper in the country and undoubtedly the worst.

With advancing years he was, by turns, or sometimes in double turns, since frequently these pursuits overlapped, a worker for various city papers, a staff correspondent in the World's War, a shamelessly prolific contributor of short and

long pieces to self-admitted popular magazines of the period;
a sporadic producer of signed columns; an after-dinner speaker;
a radio performer; a lecturer, speaking once in every sizable
city though finally, as he said, compelled to quit because he
didn't dare go back to any of the places previously visited and
couldn't afford to wait until new cities sprang up. Then at
last, he was what they called an actor before the moving-
picture camera. From his advent into this calling, he dated, so
he is reported to have said, the beginnings of his mental decay,
for not until he was approaching sixty and, as he confessed,
was beginning to swap his emotions for symptoms, did he
make his unexciting screen debut.

In his more active maturity he often declared—possibly in
defense of a secret sense of defeat—that he would rather put
his name to a story that would give a thrill to a million cham-
bermaids and half a million clodhoppers than to turn out a
book that through the ages would gather mold on the back
shelves of future public libraries. But he didn't achieve this
ambition, while the only things he ever wrote that endured for
more than a season were but two in number: a short, broad,
vulgarish thing called "Speaking of Operations," and a bro-
chure on the joys of moderate indulgence in alcoholic bever-
ages. This trumpery sketch had a wide circulation until the
Prohibition Amendment was re-enacted for the fourth time,
with added penalties providing death for drinking hard liquor;
making it a penal offense to mention the word, and a misdemeanor to hiccough publicly.

In all, Cobb had to his credit—or discredit—four hundred
short stories; thousands of columns of topical comment; reams
of dubious philosophic treatises, and nearly seventy published
books. While he didn't find readers for some of these, he
found a publisher for every one of them—which he always
claimed was a real achievement.

As in his more serious intents, so likewise in his diversions, did he encounter blockades. For a while, in his lighter moments, he specialized in telling darky stories, but was forced to abandon this diversion when anecdotes in any dialect were prohibited as an affront to race pride. Against natural handicaps he strove to become a capable bird shot. But here again, just when he reached the point where it was a shock to both parties concerned when he dropped a duck on the wing—a complete surprise to him as well as to the duck—the practical extinction of all wild life on this continent debarred him from further indulgence in his favorite sport.

Let it be added that the centenarian's life was not entirely without its compensations. The unrelated and, in part, unintelligible manuscripts that were discovered in the hut where he spent his last hours, furnished the facts as here related. They also furnished this decipherable scrap which would seem to strike a higher note than is struck anywhere among the other translatable portions:

"I knew, more or less casually, many of the distinguished men of my time. Disillusionment eventually came and pessimism was strengthened by the growing conviction that even among those called great there is too much of the parrot, the peacock and the wart hog, and not nearly enough of the dog and the elephant and the honeybee. Even evolution went askew in the production of our degenerated species. But at least it was given me to enjoy, in my enthusiastic and optimistic prime, what I maintain was the Golden Era of this world— a term of my own proud coining, only slightly tarnished by the fact that some deliberate plagiarist thought it up before I got around to doing so myself. I refer to the years extending, roughly, from 1900 to 1914. Within that brief but, alas, soon rudely ended era there were bracketed, I still insist, the highwater marks of national and international progress.

"Without either the threat of confiscation or the peril of proscription, but under pressure of popular opinion and sometimes even by quickening of the individual conscience, rich men began to manifest a true perception of their responsibilities as stewards over vast wealth. The vision of mankind broadened to new horizons as the immemorial difficulties of communication lessened—automobiles multiplying, good roads netting the land, the airplane becoming a practicable thing instead of a dangerous experiment, wireless perfected, the radio just around the corner and the miracle of television already quickening the womb of invention. Medical research was piling one splendid discovery on another. Ethical culture and economic idealism were shaking off their swaddling clothes. War on a cosmic scale was the remotest of mad nightmares. Taxes were incidents and not catastrophes. Taste in dress, in decoration, in architecture showed steady improvement. The standard of living was climbing. Women had got the vote but not yet the liquor habit. Even politics was trying to purify itself—after a fashion. One financial panic and one business slump befell—the ones of 1907—but both were so short-lived that during them no self-anointed messiahs were produced who undertook to restore prosperity by promising money they didn't have to people who hadn't earned it. The antique and now outlawed conception that government existed for the benefit of the citizens and not the citizens for the benefit of government was still finding favor. And looming bright and beautiful was the dawn of religious tolerance.

"In yearning retrospect I reckon the climax of this glorious epoch was reached when the Twentieth-Century Limited started running and William Jennings Bryan stopped."

It was shortly after our return from New Mexico that we all agreed that we would be better off, and certainly less worn down, if we closed up the house for the duration and moved to a hotel in New York. So I went on ahead to dig out some of the furniture which had been in storage from the East Hampton house, and with it furnish a suite.

While I was doing this Moie coped with closing the California place, planning to follow as soon as this was accomplished—the job being a Homeric one, let me add, because when Moie closes a house, it will stay as closed as any Egyptian tomb, can be dug up by archaeologists in the twenty-fifth century and then found as free from moth and rust as old King Tut, and they say he came out in the same condition as that New England farmer who, having died in the midst of a hard winter, was temporarily interred in the root cellar, but when the first thaw came gratified his widow no little by the handsomeness of his appearance for, when they finally fetched him up, she said, "Mercy sakes! Why, he come out as fresh as a herring!"

Dad was planning a hunting trip, so he in his turn would follow Moie as she had followed me. She arrived exhausted and instantly went to bed with an atrocious attack of flu. Then, day after day, we waited for the continually postponed arrival of the Giver of the Feast, old Rock of Gibraltar himself, the Pride of Paducah, the Guy.

First word came that he had not felt quite up to going on that hunting trip. Ominous! If that man did not feel up to getting out in the woods and knocking a few birds out of the sky and into the pot, then he was feeling mighty bad. Next we heard that he was in the hospital. We could not go to him. Reservations on the Chief, or any other Westbound train, were not to be had for the asking. As for flying, didn't we know that there was a war on? But 'Dolp Kosky, our guardian angel and doctor, was looking after him. 'Dolp wouldn't let anything happen to him. Then, just as Moie was well enough to sit up, a little telegram came, telling us that Dad would arrive three days later and was "feeling fine."

Moie was still under orders to keep to her room that day that Pat and I went down to the station to meet him. It was a Sunday morning, a New York October day with the air as crisp and juicy, if one may use that word about a day, as a home-grown apple fresh-plucked from a country orchard. The Twentieth-Century disgorged all its hundreds of passengers from those inimical caverns called train sheds of the Grand Central Station, into the wartime excitement and stir and movement of the great rotunda, where the massed flags make brave the rearing impersonal walls, and the crowds, the uniformed kids and their gallant families, trying so hard to march as lightly and quickly as their sons, seem all to move with one rhythm and to a music heard only in their hearts.

We waited and waited. Surely everyone was off that train, even the last inevitable lady straggler, the one who always leaves the diamond tiara under the pillow in the upper berth. And still he did not come. We were frightened. There was something very wrong. Oh! very wrong, indeed. No use telling ourselves he had missed the train in Chicago—if he missed a train in Chicago or anywhere else he was either dead or Chicago was having another fire, and Mrs. O'Leary's cow but an innocent bystander this time.

We were just about to give up, cease our vigil and go home and tell Laura. . . . Ah, tell Laura what? Then we saw him come slowly up the train shed. We saw him, but for a moment we did not recognize him. This bent old man, this slow-moving, stooped, shambling, thin, old man? When I reached him, breaking past the cord that is put up to keep the welcoming crowds off the necks of the arrivals, he took my arm and leaned hard on it. "Dad, Dad," I asked, "what is the matter? You don't look to me as though you ought to be walking."

"It is a little difficult," he told me.

"Then why are you?" I demanded. "Why didn't you let us know that you were so ill? We could have had a wheel chair for you."

"I could have ordered a wheel chair for myself," he said, "but I thought that Lolly would be here. I thought Lolly would be scared if she saw me in a chair."

We took him home and put him to bed. He never got up again.

One thing I do know about my Pa. He was a good game guy. In a lot of ways that was a grand winter for him. He suffered a lot of pain, and there were weeks of misery, but in between them he was propped up in his big chair and received. All the world came to see him. Why, there were times when the neighbors complained about the noisy parties in the Cobb apartment. Gene Buck, the lamb, was there three days out of seven. He used to come for tea, but most always could be persuaded to linger along until suppertime, supper for Gene and Dad consisting of oyster stew rushed down from the oyster bar in the Grand Central, and lots of crackers. A couple of bucketfuls of crackers was the usual order.

Then Pat, demure but firm according to her way, walked in one fine day, and said she rather thought she was going down to Washington that week end to marry her young man. Tableaux!

Dad called me in for a consultation. "Look here," he said, "you aren't going to let that baby get married, are you? Why, she ought to be playing with dolls! It's ridiculous!"

"All right," I said. "I will tell her that we refuse our permission. And then, after we have denied her the right to be a sailor's wife, and he goes off to the seven seas and something maybe happens to him, and she turns to me and says, 'If it

had not been for you, why, I would have had something anyhow' . . . well, on that day *you* are going to be the one to tell
her the bad news."

"Now, look here, Buff," he said. "You know I couldn't do
that."

"Neither could I," I said. "And that's exactly why I can't
tell her she can't get married either."

So it was with his blessing that Pat and I went down to
Washington to meet Greg Bautzer. Before we left he suggested that if we had a spare hour or so that we might go up
to the Capitol and call on Senator Chandler and Senator Harry
Byrd. I said that I thought it was unlikely that these eminent
gentlemen would receive a visit from us this trip, since from
here it looked as though both of us, but especially Pat, might
be pretty busy.

We were under orders to call him every hour, on the hour,
and report progress. Greg was the faithfulest about this. I
verily believe that the boy didn't take a deep breath without
reaching for the phone and telling Dad. And every time anybody called, Dad listened to the news and then asked us if we
had been to see Senator Byrd or Senator Chandler yet. Finally,
some five minutes before we were due at the church, I called
for the ultimate time. And, just before hanging up, he asked
me, "By the way, how's Senator Chandler?"

"Look, Ivy," I said, "I'm afraid that you are suffering from a
miscomprehension. Pat is not marrying Happy Chandler. She
is marrying Greg Bautzer. And all things considered, he's doing fine."

When I came back to New York, I was in a fine, exalted,
out-of-this-world and highly emotional state. And from time
to time I wept a little. I wasn't weeping about anything in
particular; the tears just seemed to roll out of my face quite
of their own accord. Over and over I told and retold every

detail of the wedding, and he as hungry to hear as I eager to recount. Then finally he rolled over in his bed and grinned at me, the true, old, authentic, merry light in his face, and said, "Buff, you know what you look like? You look like a lightning bug that's been smoking opium."

That was about the last thing he did say to me. The next day I left for California to attend to some important business for him, and two weeks later he had slid into a coma, and from it out of life.

As I write this I have been traveling back to the time, almost a year ago now, when I sat on the floor in the dusty closet in the empty house on San Vicente Boulevard. Really I have traveled farther than that, for I have been clear back to the days before I was born or thought of, and have dug deeper than I ever did to find the manuscript in the dressmaker's box. Again I have made a pilgrimage. Perhaps I found my father, and perhaps I know nothing more about him than when I started. After all, it is no news to me that he was high-tempered and kindly, that his word was his bond, that he never forgot an injury nor ever failed to forgive one. All this I knew. So now, in my mind's eye I can see him as he would be looking at me, his eyes twinkling, but shaking his head at me all the same, and I know what he would be saying. "Listen, my child, a proper respect is the thing we want cultivated around these parts. And as for your old Pa . . . he's too deep for you. And always was."

The day after I found his manuscript his last letter appeared in the papers. I think his good-by is well said by him himself.

"To Whom It May Concern:

In death I desire that no one shall look upon my face and once more I charge my family, as already and repeatedly I have done, that they shall put on none of the bogus habiliments of so-called mourning. Folds of black crepe never ministered to the memory of the departed; they only made the wearers unhappy and self-conscious.

I ask that my body be wrapped in a plain sheet or cloth and placed in an inexpensive container and immediately cremated—without any special formality or ceremony. If anybody tries to insert me into one of those dismal numbers run up by the undertaker's dressmaking department, I'll come back and ha'nt 'em. Nor do I crave to make my mortal exit in a tail-coat with white tie and artificial pearl studs. I'll be done with after-dinner speaking forever, so why dispatch me hence in the regalia of the craft? When a man dies with his sins let the sins die with the man. That's what I say and it sums up such speculations as I might ever have had touching on the future state, if any. For me a suitable epitaph would be: "Anyhow, He Left Here." But never mind that. It might offend some of the pious and I hate to go on giving offense after I've quit living.

When convenience suits, I ask that the plain canister—nothing fancy there, please—containing my ashes shall be taken to Paducah, and that at the proper planting season a hole shall be dug in our family lot or elsewhere at Oak Grove and a dogwood tree planted there and the ashes strewn in the hole to fertilize the tree roots. Should the tree live that will be monument enough for me. But should my surviving relatives desire to mark the spot further, I make so bold as to suggest that they use either a slab of plain Kentucky limestone set flat in the kindly earth, or a rugged natural boulder of Southern granite bearing a small bronze plate with my name on it and, if it seems pertinent, the year of my birth and the year of my death, which appears to be the custom although I could never understand why a gravestone should carry mention of the only two events in the career of the deceased with which he had absolutely nothing to do—unless he committed suicide. Also on the bronze tablet or the stone slab as the case may be, and provided it doesn't cost too much, I'd like to have inscribed certain lines from the epitaph which Robert Louis Stevenson wrote for himself, to wit as follows:

> "This be the verse you grave for me:
> Here he lies where he longed to be;
> Home is the sailor, home from sea,
> And the hunter home from the hill."

I'm quoting from memory. If I'm wrong will somebody kindly correct me?

Or, if a simpler single line bearing the same imprint seems desirable, I offer this one as suitable: "I Have Come Back Home."

And, thank you, no flowers. Does anybody feel moved to send flowers, I'd prefer that they give the money they'd spend there to some local non-denominational charity. Cover the spot with leaves—Christmas berries from the flatlands and cedar from the friendly low McCracken County ridges if it be winter, and leafy boughs from native hickories or hackberries or wild crab-apples if it be in other seasons.

Above all I want no long faces and no show of grief at the burying ground. Kindly observe the final wishes of the undersigned and avoid reading the so-called Christian burial service which, in view of the language employed in it, I regard as one of the most cruel and paganish things inherited by our forebears from our remote pagan ancestors. In deference to the faith of our dear mother who was through her lifetime a loyal though never bigoted communicant of that congregation, perhaps the current pastor of the First Presbyterian Church would consent to read the Twenty-third Psalm, which was her favorite passage in the Scriptures and is mine since it contains no charnel words, no morbid mouthings about corruption and decay and, being mercifully without creed or dogma, carries no threat of eternal hell-fire for those parties we do not like, no direct promise of a heaven which, if one may judge by the people who are surest of going there, must be a powerfully dull place, populated to a considerable and uncomfortable degree by prigs, time-servers and unpleasantly aggressive individuals. Hell may have a worse climate but undoubtedly the company is sprightlier. The Catholics, with their genius for stage-management, handle this detail better. The officiating clergyman speaks in Latin and the parishioners, being unacquainted with that language, are impressed by the mystery and the majesty of the rolling, sonorous periods without being shocked by distressing allusions and harrowing references.

As an aside I might add that my notion of an ideal religion would combine the dignity and the beauty of the Romanist ritual with certain other ingredients; the good taste and the ability of the Unitarians and Episcopalians—a trait not too common to some of the Evangelical groups—to mind their own business. (I'm proud that I never set myself up to be My Brother's Keeper, having been sufficiently occupied by the job of being my own keeper.) To these add the noble ethics and the splendid tolerances expressed in Reformed Judaism; the sturdy independence and the good business principles of the Mormons; the gentle humility and orderly humanity of the Quakers, plus the militant zeal and unselfish devotion of those Shock Troops of the Lord—the Salvation Army, who fight in the trenches of Sin's No Man's Land to reclaim the tortured souls and clothe the naked bodies of those whom the rest of a snobbish world forgot. If, based on this combination, there was a determination to practice the sectless preachments and the teachings of Jesus Christ, who was the first true gentleman of recorded history and the greatest gentleman that ever lived, I might not have joined the fold but certainly I'd have stood on the side lines and cheered for it. By the way, have you ever noticed that in time of war not the most passionate partisan dares to ask the Prince of Peace to bless his bloody arms and forward his bloody deeds? He invokes the aid of the God of unjustified battles as created by the ancient Hebrews. All Hitler needed to do was let his whiskers sprout and sit on a nest of thunderbolts and naked swords, thinking up plague and pestilence and rapine and slaughter and slavery for the vanquished, to be a fit understudy for the vengeful murderous Jehovah of the forepart of the Old Testament. For Brother Joe Stalin, our present beloved ally and, secretly, the everlasting enemy of our institutions, the job would be easier. He already has the whiskers. (One advantage of dying is that it affords a fellow opportunity to say a lot of things that have been curdling in his system all these years. Frankly, I'm enjoying myself.)

But getting back to what I was talking about: I am a life member of Paducah Lodge, No. 217, B. P. O. E. But I'd prefer that the burial program of the order not be read. Like most burial programs it needs editing. However, if the members desire to turn out, either as a body or singly, I'll be very glad to have them present. Judging by my latest visits to the basement of the Elks' Club it wouldn't do them a bit of harm if some of the habitués there got out in the open air if only for a trip to a cemetery.

For the wind-up I'd be grateful if some of my colored friends sang, first "Swing Low, Sweet Chariot" and then "Deep River." I think I could count on Mattie Copeland of Jones Street, who for so many years was a loyal, loving servant of my family, to recruit the singers from the choirs of our colored churches.

I was almost overlooking one item: I take it that there will be no need for pallbearers, as the trade term goes. Pallbearers are another surviving relic of heathen practices. Recalling how this pair of my friends could cuddle to their bosoms three of a kind in a dollar-limit game, I'd nominate either George Goodman or Will Gilbert as a dependable custodian of my mortal remainders on the trip to the burying-ground. Anyhow, properly rendered down, my ashes shouldn't much more than fill a Mason fruit jar.

Among others I'd like to invite to go along for the ride—provided they promise to be cheerful and bright—I think of Colonel Gus Thompson, Fred Neuman, Herbert Wallerstein, Jim Smith, Douglas Bagby, Ed Paxton, Captain Louis Igert, Fletch Terrell, Ed Scott, Jim English, Henry Weil, A. R. Meyers, Dr. Warren Sights, Dr. Frank Boyd, Linn Boyd, Roy Nelson, Tom Waller, Jack Fisher, Roy McKinney, James D. Langstaff, Morton Hand, Henry Ward, Leo Keiler, Elliott Mitchell, Rev. Custis Fletcher, Luther Carson, James Langstaff, Charley Vahlkamp, Wade Sowell, Bob Moshell and Charley Beard. If I have overlooked any suitable candidates I beg their pardon. Ladies also welcome with or without escorts.

I rather figure some of my fellow townspeople might favor memorial exercises of sorts, either in connection with the funeral or elsewhere. Personally I have no objection, only desiring that no dismal note be permitted to ooze into the proceedings. Keep the thing cheerful, boys and girls. If somebody feels called upon to speak, I'd like to suggest for the job—well, say, Tom Waller. He could be depended upon to be neither verbose nor lachrymose. Or if Waller isn't available there's Jack Fisher or Jim Wheeler or Roy Shelbourne. Only, make it snappy.

Well, I reckon that will be about all except that I extend, in passing, my affectionate and grateful regards to the gracious and generous folk who make up so overwhelmingly the dwellers in my home community, and my native section. You've been mighty good to me and I appreciate it. Much obliged, you-all, and good-by and bless you and prosper you.

(Signed)

IRVIN S. COBB.

At New York,
December, 1943.